Soul
Companion

Soul
Companion
A Memoir

Judy Hilyard, RN, MN

Anam Cara Companion

Published by Anam Cara Companion
Ashland, Oregon

www.anamcaracompanion.com

Softbound ISBN: 978-0-578-64578-0

Hardbound ISBN: 978-0-578-68681-3

eBook ISBN: 978-0-578-68687-5

Cover art: Jan Alexander/Pixabay

Author photo: Debra Thornton, www.debrathornton.com

Book Design and Production
by Lucky Valley Press
Jacksonville Oregon
www.luckyvalleypress.com

Printed in the United States of America
on acid-free paper.

Contents

Acknowledgements

As anyone who has ever written a book knows, it takes at least a village.... I have many people for whom I have great gratitude. First, to my writers' group, The Assisi Mystery School, for giving me feedback on the many drafts of each chapter over a five year period—Shoshana Alexander, our skilled coach who convinced me to write a memoir, and writers Bill Kastenberg, Barbara Shor and Carolyn Shaffer.

Connie Crow did an in-depth first edit of the manuscript. I asked several of my friends to read the manuscript and give me feedback, all very helpful—Jude Corbin, Susan Edmonds, Jerrye Wright, Elin Babcock, Ronda Barker, Jean Bakewell, Kay Cutter, Sandie Black, Rebecca Kay, Pam Derby, Kathy Apple, and Nancy Wynkoop.

I wish to honor Mike and Elin Babcock for their deep generosity. I am very grateful to Ginna and David Gordon at Lucky Valley Press who took my manuscript, did much more editing, and made it into this book.

Debra Thornton, of Debra Thornton Photography, took wonderful photos of Puffin and me for the book cover. Thank you, Debra.

Thank you all, for your help and support as I, in Shoshana's words, first became a writer and then an author.

Preface

This preface will end well. I promise it will. This book is joyful, with astonishing, life-expanding, jaw-dropping adventures you will not want to miss. But, I start here—

There was a time, almost five decades ago, when I was a 28-year-old head nurse of a coronary intensive care unit. The hospital was a prestigious and innovative place to work and I loved my job, the staff and doctors, and especially our patients and their families.

One ordinary day, we admitted Paul to our unit, a 45-year-old man with a life-threatening heart rhythm problem. The paramedics had shocked his heart back into a normal rhythm at his home and then again several times in the ambulance as his wife, Joanne, sat by his side. His heart kept going back into ventricular tachycardia—a rhythm that would not sustain his life more than a few minutes. Over the next few days, we had to shock his heart several more times, before the doctors were able to come up with the right combination of medications to keep him in a normal rhythm.

However, Paul was re-admitted to our unit every few months for the next two years for the same heart rhythm problem. We all came to adore Paul, a happy, funny fellow with bright blue eyes. He and Joanne had a joyful relationship, with laughter and pranks going on in his room.

And yet, he still went into the chaotic heart rhythm. He never lost consciousness as we came running into his room, pushing the defibrillator to his bedside, putting the paddles on his chest and shocking him, once or several times with each episode. He was always awake and it was very painful to endure. I have heard it is like being kicked in the chest by a horse. I have never been defibrillated but I *have* been kicked by a horse. It was painful!

Paul occasionally became less aware (as his body was not getting oxygen) until we could get him back into a normal heart rhythm. When we did get him back to a regular heartbeat, he joked about the experience.

This was a time long before implantable defibrillators and medications that could control his heart rhythm. The only treatment that worked was defibrillation, time and time again.

Each July, a new group of residents rotated onto our unit to work alongside the cardiologists. About two years after Paul became a regular customer in our coronary ICU, a new group of resident doctors began the cardiology service. It was a time for the team of doctors to review the medical records of our frequently admitted patients and decide on any new approaches to their care. The head resident would let me know about the new approaches for each of the returning patients.

I was shocked when it came to Paul. The team of doctors decided that the next time he was admitted to our unit, we were *not* to defibrillate him when he went into his chaotic heart rhythm. We were to let him die. The reason was that over those two years his heart had gotten more and more damaged and there was nothing in medicine or surgery that could help Paul. His only option was death—sooner or later.

I could not accept that plan! I went to the chief cardiologist to present my case for Paul. But the chief agreed with the plan. Nothing more could be done to save Paul's life.

This was also a time in our cultural history when patients were generally not told their diagnosis or that they were going to die. This was true in Paul's case. He was not told that we would not defibrillate him. And we were not to tell him. His wife knew the plan but was also not to tell him. How hard that must have been for her!

I could not imagine giving any of our RNs the terrible responsibility of staying at Paul's bedside and not running to get the defibrillator to shock him back to life. It was too much to ask. As the head nurse, I didn't take patient assignments so I could manage the whole unit, but I decided to take Paul as my patient the next time he was admitted.

And so I did, some weeks later. Paul had been defibrillated at home by the paramedics and admitted to our unit, as usual. I assigned him to me.

A couple of days later, while I was caring for him, he went back into that chaotic rhythm. I stood at his bedside and held his hand. Paul looked up at me with his beautiful blue eyes and anxiously said, "Judy, go get the defibrillator!" He said it several times, pleading with me to defibrillate him. I kept saying, "It is going to be OK, Paul." But it was definitely not okay with me. I could not get the defibrillator because of the doctor's orders. I would have done it anyway if I had really disagreed with the plan—but I didn't disagree. I knew we could not save our beloved Paul—in the end, we could not keep him alive.

So, I just stood there, holding his hand and saying it was going to be OK. I listened to Paul beg me to go get the defibrillator. I looked into his eyes—and did not tell him I was letting him die. It seemed to take an eternity for him to lose consciousness. He finally did stop breathing and that chaotic rhythm came to an end. Joanne came in a few minutes later and understood what had happened. She was broken hearted, as were all of the staff—as was I.

I carried that guilt and pain of Paul's death until December of 2012. At the time, I was in a place called the Monroe Institute in Virginia, to learn how to go to the Other Side of the Veil—the veil that separates our physical lives from physical death and whatever comes after that. All of this is explained in detail in *Soul Companion, A Memoir*.

But right now, I want to share how my guilt and pain over Paul's death evaporated on my second day at the Institute. We were learning how to experience greatly expanded levels of awareness and consciousness as we listened to specifically created CDs which helped us get into a deep meditative state. Guided by Robert Monroe's voice on the CD, we went to an expanded level of awareness he called Focus 15, where we would experience—no time—or all time—or past, present and future—all together.

As I took my first trip to that extraordinary level of awareness of "No Time–All Time," I saw two people standing on a vibrant, shimmering, white bridge. They also shimmered with Golden Light—Light so brilliant I thought I would melt. They seemed familiar but were much less dense than people in physical bodies. These two Beautiful, Joyful Beings were laughing. As I came closer to them, there was handsome blued-eyed Paul and his joyful, radiant wife, Joanne. They were waiting for me—for me! They embraced me. I never felt so unconditionally loved and held before in my life. But I wasn't exactly in my life—I was in a place beyond this physical existence and beyond this Earth.

As I was held and loved by them, Paul and Joanne told me I was not at fault for Paul's death; that they had planned what would happen in Paul's life before they each came into that lifetime. Paul's life and death happened just as they had planned it. And I was part of the planning—each of us met on the Other Side before we were born into this lifetime. We planned that whole part of our lives together—where we would intersect and how I would lovingly support Paul in his death.

I stayed in the loving, joyful presence of Paul and Joanne for some time and then, Robert Monroe's voice directed us back to this time and this space—back to the Monroe Institute and December 2012.

I came out of that experience sobbing, with wave upon wave of gratitude for the release of decades of guilt and pain over my handling of Paul's death. Paul and Joanne took it from me that day. I understood Paul's death at a deeper level than ever before.

There is more Healing, Love, Joy, Peace and Freedom to come in the pages of *Soul Companion*. I hope you enjoy it as much as I am enjoying sharing it. And I hope you have less fear of death and dying for having read it.

Judy Hilyard, RN, MN
February, 2020
Ashland, Oregon

Chapter 1
No Longer Lost

Jim paces around on an abandoned battlefield, mumbling to himself. As I view the field to the horizon in all directions, it is dirt brown and littered with war machinery in all stages of brokenness. There are small columns of smoke slowly rising from scattered areas on the field. The air and sky have a gray-brown hue. In a frenzied manner, Jim moves between machinery and the burned and fallen trees, continually repeating to himself, "I don't want to die. I don't want my body in pieces."

This was the beginning of my time with Jim on the Other Side of the Veil that separates this existence from the Afterlife.

It was January of 2013 and I was at the Monroe Institute in Virginia, a participant in the Lifeline program. I was in my isolation booth with headphones on, listening to a Hemi-Synchronization CD broadcasting to all 21 of us taking that Monroe program. We each had an isolation booth and were connected to our facilitators by the headphones. The CD helped us into a deep meditative state where we could be aware of an existence beyond normal consciousness.

Our work in this Monroe program was to find people who had died but were caught up in a kind of mind-loop and didn't know they were physically dead. They were alone and trapped

in an in-between space or dimension. Our two facilitators prepared us the previous day to retrieve Souls that had died but
were stuck in a space Robert Monroe called Focus 23.

The facilitators said we needed to be able to do two things
when we met these trapped Souls. First, get their attention
because they were caught in a mind-loop and would have a
hard time noticing anything outside their own mental imagin-
ings. Second, give them a compelling reason to come with us
to a place where they could get help.

Jim was the first person I encountered during that
expanded awareness process and the first person I was able
to retrieve and move to the very loving and creative level of
existence in the Afterlife called Focus 27.

Jim, and the place where I saw him, were incredibly vivid
to me although it was not in what we could experience in
normal awareness. I experienced myself on that battlefield.
I could see the destruction all around me. I could smell the
smoldering fires. There were no sounds I was aware of—
more of an eerie stillness. I sensed that if I took a step, the
dirt under my feet would billow up around me, a fine dirty dust
that seemed to cover everything. I knew I was not in a physical environment but it felt very real.

I recognized Jim as a patient I took care of in an intensive care unit (ICU) in Connecticut 46 years earlier. I didn't
remember why he was in the ICU but I vividly remembered
him and his frantic way of being. Jim was frightened of everything—people, pills, bed linens and IV bottles. He shook and
quivered and reacted with panic to almost any interaction.

At the time I took care of Jim, I was a new nurse in my
early twenties. I was a stoic New Englander. I couldn't understand or appreciate Jim's high level of fear and nervousness.
And then, one day he told me his story and that changed
everything for me.

He was a private in the army during World War II. His job

was to go onto battlefields after the battles and pick up what he could find of American soldiers, sometimes a whole body, but more often, body parts. This psychologically damaged him too greatly to fulfill any future life he might have wanted.

As I arrived on the battlefield to connect with Jim, I had two Guides with me, my white Arabian horse, Ben and my white Samoyed dog, Kismet. Both of them died years before but had come forward during my training to assist me in retrieving Souls. Our facilitators asked us to invite helpers from the Other Side to be with us in this work. It didn't surprise me that they would show up to help because I had a deep and loving connection with both of them during their lives.

A third Guide who came forward at my request was a Being I called Samantha. She didn't seem to have a name. I thought maybe it was because her function was more universal than individual. She was very gentle and loving and new to me. Samantha would be in Focus 27 to meet me when I arrived with those I retrieved. She would take them to wherever they needed to go next. What I would find out later at the Monroe Institute was that any guides and helpers who do come forward are very likely to be guides who have known us and have been with us forever. That included Ben and Kismet.

As Ben, Kismet and I appear on the battlefield, Jim is shocked to see a white horse and a white dog. He says, "What are these animals doing here? They could get hurt and they are certainly going to get dirty."

I tell him that we are there to help him. Jim lets out a deep breath, as if he is starting to relax.

As his shoulders begin to drop, he says to me, "I am exhausted and I want to find some place to sit down. There is nothing to sit down on here without getting covered with dirt."

I explain, "I can take you to a place where you can really rest, if you would like."

"Yes, ma'am, I would love that. Thank you for your kindness."

While we are talking, Jim is closely eyeing my horse, Ben. I tell him he may ride Ben to where we are going. He jumps up onto Ben and we go to Focus 27.

Samantha is there to meet us. Jim hops off of Ben and salutes Samantha, saying, "What are you doing here, Sir?" My understanding is that Jim sees Samantha as an officer from his platoon.

During my time with Jim and all the others since then, I understand immediately what a person is thinking, feeling and saying while I am in the expanded level of awareness. Robert Monroe called it *non-verbal communication* and it works no matter what language the person spoke during their lifetime. There is nothing hidden on the Other Side of this reality. Thoughts, feelings and intentions are transmitted without barrier or time delay.

Samantha tells Jim she is there to help. As she says that, fanning out behind her as far as I could see, American soldiers in uniform come into view and all salute Jim at once. The awareness comes to me that these are soldiers whose bodies or body parts had been retrieved by Jim in his work during World War II.

I stand to the side of Jim. I can see him, Samantha and all of the soldiers saluting him. I weep with Compassion and Understanding for him and all those dead soldiers. Jim seems stunned by their recognition of his service. Tears roll down his face, leaving streaks of clean white skin under the dirt accumulated on the battlefield. In time, all of the soldiers surround Jim and escort him to a beautiful Healing Center.

The scene faded and I was back in my isolation booth. As I came out of that expanded awareness there were tears running down my cheeks. The love and compassion I felt for Jim was deeper than any I could remember in my life up to that time. I was moved by the honor and gratitude given to Jim by the soldiers. It was the first of hundreds of experiences I have witnessed of a depth of love, understanding and compassion demonstrated by Beings on the Other Side of this Time and this Space.

The chapters to follow will describe my journey from the person I was to who I am now—a *Soul Companion*. It has been a winding journey, as life journeys usually are for us Humans. I am grateful! And it will end wonderfully!

Chapter 2
A Celtic Shock

"When you came here a few days ago, you were broken hearted. Now you are broken open," John said. He was right on both counts. I sat beside this kind social worker all four days of the beginning of an apprenticeship in the Anam Cara tradition. We were learning an ancient way of working with the dying, a practice developed in sixth-century Celtic Europe, that would one day be known as Hospice Care. Little did I know that first day I was being broken open to a new life.

"Anam Cara" is a Celtic term meaning "Soul Friend," a loving companion, friend and guide who walks with another through their challenges and concerns as they prepare for death. It was a common custom among the Celts for an Anam Cara to companion a person as they resolved the grief of a lifetime in order to enter a peaceful death. These ancient roles were revived and developed into a modern-day approach by Richard Groves, founder of the Sacred Art of Living Center that teaches how to discover the sacred in all aspects of life. Richard, his wife Mary and John O'Donohue, the noted Irish poet, author, philosopher and scholar, created the Anam Cara apprenticeship together.

That first day of the workshop about sixty of us were entering a two-year apprenticeship. Ours was the first site of three in the United States and one in Ireland beginning the apprenticeship within weeks of each other that year. At the front of our meeting room on either side of the lectern where Richard stood, were four six-foot-high reproductions of Celtic art representing the four pillars of the Anam Cara tradition: soulfulness, skillfulness, community and mentorship. I studied these images over the subsequent days, finding each touched my heart. One in particular attracted me—a depiction of Bridget of Kildare who lived in the sixth century CE and was considered to be a bridge between the new Christian religion taking hold in Celtic lands and the older, Earth-based spirituality of the Celts. She was known to the Celtic people as a Druid princess, and to the new religion as a Christian saint. Bridget was considered to be one of the first Anam Caras in the land. Richard told us a few of the legends about her abilities. As I studied that representation of Bridget, she looked into my Soul.

* * *

A few weeks before, a sixteen-year relationship with my partner and deep spiritual friend had ended. It was a complex union that left me with complicated grief I had not yet begun to sort out. Though the partnership produced for me great highs and lows, it also supported my compelling Belief that we were sharing a spiritual quest. For us, that quest involved a number of trips together to Chartres, France—to the beloved and famous twelfth century Chartres Cathedral. With my first step onto the land and into the cathedral I felt a deep Knowing that this was "Home," a home I had never experienced before. At the time I did not understand what that meant but I knew it in my bones, and that I had experienced Chartres in a partnership that now was over.

A few months before entering the Anam Cara apprenticeship, I completed another two-year program with Richard called "The Sacred Art of Living and Dying." In this cross-cultural course, we learned how to diagnose and treat the spiritual pain of others, particularly at the end of life. We discovered that unresolved pain related to issues of forgiveness, relationships, hope and meaning could keep people clinging to life at all costs, causing a struggle at the end of life. We also learned that this kind of spiritual pain might occur any time in one's life.

In that course, I became adept at identifying and using many different modalities to treat the spiritual pain in others. Yet now, here I was in this Anam Cara training, and all four of those pains were unresolved in me—lack of forgiveness, broken relationship, no hope or meaning in my life. How could that be? The ending of that relationship left me feeling that everything was gone, just dust. I was in great existential and spiritual pain.

I spent most of the weekend crying as Richard launched us into this two-year exploration of another way to be with the dying. Once I started crying, I could not stop. I came from stoic New England stock. I had never cried in front of a group of people before and I didn't like being so vulnerable in front of individuals I didn't know. But unlike my normal way of behaving, I had no control over my reactions. I was so broken open that everything was deeply moving to me.

I saw that the tears were not only caused by the despair I felt over the sudden ending of my relationship but also by the beautiful, heart-felt way Richard described what we would be learning and becoming in the next two years. I was touched by the exquisite beauty of a loving way to support others at the end of a physical life.

It turned out that the first year of the training focused on our own inner preparation for working with the dying, and was just what I needed. That year of inner work was very healing for me—my broken heart mended more quickly than I would have ever thought possible. One of the profound lessons I learned that first year was how to be an Anam Cara to myself. Then I would be ready to enter the second year, about building our skills in the end-of-life work with others.

* * *

During the time I was immersed in the apprenticeship, I was still in my last few years of a 47 year career in critical care nursing, focused on saving patients' lives. I taught others how to save lives by understanding the subtle and not so subtle signs and symptoms of impending physiological distress. I was in the business of keeping people from dying.

Therefore, it might have seemed a bit odd to those who knew me to hear that I was now becoming a companion and guide for people who were dying, allowing the natural process to unfold rather than trying to stop it. If I had been able to see into the future I would one day inhabit, it would have seemed odd to me as well.

I fell in love with critical care nursing. I entered it when that specialty was just developing. In the mid 1960s, the hospital in Connecticut for which I worked opened an innovative unit known as "Intensive Care" (ICU). Those of us considering working there were told we would take care of no more than two patients at a time. That would allow us to gain an in-depth knowledge of each patient and his or her disease. Therefore, we would not be juggling up to ten patients at a time per shift, a typical nursing assignment in most hospitals then. In this new specialty of medicine and nursing, I had the time to focus not only on the physical condition of patients but also on getting to know them and their families.

Because of those aspects of the work, I felt satisfied to be a staff nurse at the bedside of the critically ill. I was surprised and honored by the way intimate and therapeutic relationships could develop between nurse, patient and family in the midst of tragedy. And it was thrilling to me to participate in saving people's lives, working collaboratively with all of the disciplines within a hospital and relying on my own attention to details in the care and treatment of each patient. I became skilled in re-starting patients' hearts through defibrillation and CPR.

There were times in my early career when I felt a heady power at being able to save lives—yes, me! And all by myself at times. In a number of situations I had electrically shocked a patient's heart back into a life-sustaining rhythm before the rest of the cardiac arrest team had even arrived in the unit. I stood there with a satisfied look on my face as the team came running into the ICU only to find the patient already awake and alert.

But there were also patients I came to love whom I could not save. Nobody could. Death was the only possible outcome. That was hard for me to accept at first. But slowly that egoic satisfaction at pulling a patient back from the jaws of death was replaced by reality and some degree of acceptance of the inevitability of death.

As a dedicated critical care nurse, I was passionate to learn as much as I could about the physical body and the disease processes that created problems for that body. In my quest to learn about those complexities, I went back to school and earned both a bachelor's and a master's degree in nursing. As this placed me in the position to assume additional responsibilities in administrative roles, I returned to school again for a Masters in Administration. I was well-trained in the Western Medicine approach to treating illness and saving lives.

While I greatly appreciated this knowledge and approach, slowly I realized that almost nothing in my education, training or practice prepared me to assist my patients in a peaceful death. Something was amiss about saving a life no matter the cost—physical, emotional, mental or financial. During my last few years at the bedside, it became increasingly difficult to feel right about participating in the treatment plan created for patients with a very slim chance of surviving even long enough to move out of the ICU. If they did survive, they frequently died before being discharged from the hospital. With the focus only on living, so many of my patients who died did so with no preparation for death at all.

I felt it was inappropriate that this was the only approach for those moving into the last weeks, days or hours of life. Many of those patients were almost entirely alone, comatose, in an unfamiliar environment and assaulted by multiple invasive interventions with no opportunity to be ready for the great transition from life to... whatever was on the Other Side of that life. I wondered if this was a total shock for them. Did they find their way to... elsewhere? Did all our life-sustaining interventions hinder their dying process to the extent that they were lost when their physical body no longer lived? I was participating in staving off death for some people but not preparing them for the inevitable. Was this right? I needed answers to those questions.

When I heard about the Anam Cara apprenticeship with Richard, I was interested in how I might learn this different way of working with the dying. Though I had been raised a Christian, during the previous two decades of my nursing career I was a spiritual seeker. Something about the Anam Cara work called to me and I signed up without a moment's hesitation. Right from the beginning of the training, a new vision emerged in my life for how to proceed with end-of-life care.

* * *

So I found myself sitting next to John during the first hour of the first of day of the first year of the Anam Cara apprenticeship. Richard was reviewing the tradition of Anam Cara.

He had covered this practice during the training I had just completed with him. I remember thinking I wasn't going to learn anything new that hour.

But then he added a few sentences I had not heard him say before. "In early Celtic times, there were some Anam Caras who had a special ability. They could not only walk with someone *to* dying, they could walk with someone *through* dying. They could escort a person to the Other Side of the Veil. A person who could do this was called an Anam Aira, a person who cares for the Soul."

I could hear Richard going on with his talk, but I was stopped-still. I had been hit with a bolt of lightning, suddenly aware of something I felt destined to do—something I hadn't even known existed until that instant. I desired to know how to do *that*, to escort someone across the Veil from living to dying.

At lunchtime I was still reeling from the introduction of this new idea, but as I talked with and listened to my fellow apprentices, no one else seemed to even be aware of this incredible bit of information shaking me to my core. I was the only one shocked into that desire. Richard didn't mention any more about Anam Aira. Looking back on that day, I might have asked him more about Anam Aira at a break or lunch but I was just too stunned.

Later in the year, when I did ask Richard about the concept of Anam Aira, he told me about *A Celtic Book of Dying: Watching with the Dying, Traveling with the Dead*, by Phyllida Anam Aire. She had been trained at her mother's knee to do this Anam Aira work. After reading the book, I looked her up on the internet and found she had moved from the Celtic lands to focus on creating music in Germany. I tried to contact her through her publisher but never heard back. It was clear I would need to discover how to do this sacred work on my own.

A couple of years later, I was in Kildare, Ireland, with Richard, walking the land that Bridget of Kildare walked. I remembered how focused I had been on the banner of Bridget during the two years of the Anam Cara Apprenticeship. On a rainy, wind-blown day we stood in the ruins of a church that tradition said was built by Bridget. I was enthralled as Richard related stories of Bridget, doing the work of not only the first Anam Cara but also the first Anam Aira in history. Maybe I was drawn to that towering image of Bridget in our conference room because she would become my guide in Anam Aira work.

* * *

With the utterance of those few sentences about Anam Aira, Richard had broken my heart open to the possibility of a completely new way of being in service to others. It would take me a few days during that first session of the apprenticeship to move from shocked attention to understanding there was something extremely important I needed to know. I needed to know how to be an Anam Aira.

During those four days of the training and through my tears, my heart opened more and more. My crushed spirit slowly engaged in life again. My curiosity woke up. How was I going to learn how to do something that may not have been practiced for many centuries, something completely outside of my knowledge of critical care nursing or even my world view? I didn't know how, but I did know I would find a way. I had to know how to escort people over to the Other Side of the Veil at their moment of death. I had no idea why that desire had arisen in me.

But before I could learn how to be an Anam Aira, there was a significant journey to take and dots to connect along the way.

Chapter 3
A Long Journey

Journeys are often detours placed end to end. As a shy 20-year-old, I had no idea of the roller coaster life headed my way—none of us do. These are the detours that began my Anam Aira journey.

For many of the early decades of my life, I imagined having the skill to see difficult situations from a broader perspective. For any situation that gave me a heartache or perplexed me, I wanted to "jump up" high and look at the problem from 28,000 feet—to see beyond the trivial details. Instead of being able to do that, mired *in* the details, I frequently felt the pain, the slights, the knot of resentment. What I really wanted to know was what any troubling situation meant in a larger scheme of things. Sadly, no matter my desire, I didn't know how to do that. Then, that ability miraculously came to pass for me during the late 1990s. It was glorious. And temporary.

At that time, my life partner (the same partner I lost weeks before the Anam Cara apprenticeship) and I decided to walk the five-hundred-mile Camino of Santiago De Compostela in Spain. The night before our first day of walking the Camino, we were in Roncesvalles, at the top of the Pyrenees Mountain Range—one of the traditional places where pilgrims start the Camino and walk 500 hundred miles due West. I barely made it up the three flights of stairs with my heavy backpack, falling, with heaving breaths, onto the first open bunk bed in a big sweeping room with row upon row of three-tier bunks. We were to sleep with a hundred other pilgrims before taking the first steps on the famed Path. To say I was not physically fit is an understatement, as I was at least one hundred pounds heavier than most people walking the Camino. I practiced walking—maybe a couple of miles at a time—for just a week before starting the pilgrimage. Over the next seven weeks, it was a very hard trek for me, physically, emotionally and mentally.

When my partner and I finally reached the outskirts of Santiago, we looked down at the city and the famed cathedral from a place called The Mount of Joy. I felt that "jumping up" phenomenon I wished for earlier in life. Initially, I felt a sense of expansion of my mind and perceptions. It seemed like my third eye chakra in my forehead opened up and everything was—lighter—less heavy but also there was a lightness—as in brightness—an ability to see what I couldn't "see" before.

From that moment at the Mount of Joy and lasting several weeks, I awakened to the broader meaning of things—large concepts like how the whole Universe worked and small concepts such as the far-reaching cosmic meaning of staying in a hotel in Santiago named The Universe.

One of the outcomes of this new ability was the understanding of a verse in the Bible that had always baffled me: "In the beginning was the Word and the Word was with God and the Word was God." I *knew* what that meant! I understood what the Word was and that expanded my understanding of ALL THERE IS. For weeks after the Mount of Joy, no matter what happened to me, I knew and understood it all at a deeper level. I felt joy, peace and gratitude.

For years, astronomy, cosmology and quantum physics had fascinated me. As new books came out on these subjects, I devoured them—books from authors such as Brian Green, Michael Talbot, Steven Hawking and Larry Dossey. Did I understand all of it? No, not at all, but I was forever captivated by the interconnection that was present in the Universe.

Now, activated on the Mount of Joy, all my wonderings were answered spontaneously, without even a sense of a question about why, what, how and who. I understood how the Universe was created, how it continued to transform, and the amazing interconnection of All. I was given a language to describe it—a way of expressing this *Knowingness*. It all seemed so simple. How could so many have missed it? How could I have missed it?

I lived in Portland, Oregon at the time. That insight lasted for a couple of weeks after returning to the hustle and bustle of the city and resuming my work as a clinical nurse special-ist in cardiology in a large hospital. It didn't matter that I had to move back into functioning with my honed left brain thinking because I could still appreciate the broader context of everything. It was just there for me and it would always be there. Sadly, I didn't write any of this new *Knowingness* down.

One day, I woke up in the morning and the *knowing* was gone. All of the ability to *know*, see, understand and articu-late how the whole Process and Universe worked was totally absent. I felt empty. And alone.

For years I tried to figure out how to get that ability back. It was not just that I didn't know those important answers any more. I also felt alone, empty of something I could not articulate.

Years later, I asked Gangaji, a spiritual leader I valued, if I could get it back. She said that first, it would be good to just be grateful for having had that awareness because most people do not. She also said the information, the knowledge, the wisdom was still in my Being. It had not left me—only my awareness of it had changed. Her explanation gave me some hope but did not answer my question about how to reconnect with that blissful expansive consciousness.

The desire to understand issues from a broader perspective stayed with me, but I thought less about how to get the *Knowingness* back. The answer, the catalyst for the answer, came in 2012. I saw a movie called *The Way* by Emilio Estevez, starring his father, Martin Sheen. It was based on a true story about a father who walked the Santiago Camino for his son who had fallen to his death in the foggy Pyrenees Mountains on his first day of the Camino.

I was hooked again, wanting to walk the Camino one more time in my life. I desired to walk it gracefully rather than whining and complaining as I had the first time. I wanted to be fit enough to walk without great physical duress. The Mount of Joy experience came to mind but I didn't want to set up expectations. My focus was to get in good physical shape for a "Buen Camino"—a Good Way.

I started training in the spring, planning to leave the middle of September with two friends. During the spring and summer, as I walked the trails around my home in Ashland, I was eighty pounds lighter than I had been the last time. I would train for months this time. However, I also developed a heart rhythm irregularity in those ensuing years. I was short of breath going up hills, even with less weight. But I was determined to be ready.

There was another weight I also wanted to let go of that summer. I wanted to forgive my father for something that happened over forty years earlier, something I had carried since I was twenty-five years old. I wanted to lay that burden down, for me and for my 88 year old father.

* * *

I grew up in a fundamentalist, evangelical church, where many activities were considered sinful—going to movies, dancing, playing cards, roller-skating to music and wearing lipstick, to name a few. I was a very devout child and followed that belief system without question.

But I knew I was different. I didn't find boys interesting and had no attraction to them when many of my girlfriends were talking about nothing else. I was attracted to my Sunday school teacher or my gym teacher or the choir director—all female. I never said anything about this to anyone because I knew it would be bad news for me. I heard about how sinful it was to be a homosexual. In our church, it was pretty much the worst sin a person could commit. Even though I didn't really know what a homosexual was, I felt like I might be one. None of my friends were talking about being in love with our Sunday school teacher, Beatrice—they were talking about being in love with the boys who sat next to them in Sunday school class.

This caused me great concern, so I tried not to think about it. As a shy and introverted girl, I had one close friend. I lived in the same town until I was fourteen. After that, we moved several times until I finished high school. But all through grade school and high school, I harbored feelings of undeclared and unrequited crushes for several older women in my life.

After high school, I entered nursing school, a three-year residential program. It was September of 1963. I lived in a dorm with twenty-four other nursing students. All through nursing school, I dated a nice fellow I met while working for my father in a slipper factory the summer before I started nursing school. Hector and his family were refugees who emigrated from Cuba during the early years of Castro's rule.

Hector was almost as shy as I was and he never even kissed me until the day of my graduation from nursing school.

And on that day, he proposed. I said yes. I felt like I was on the right track. I was not different any more. But, truth be told, I had more of a crush on Hector's mother than I did on him. But I didn't tell that Truth, not even to myself, except in the secret hours of the night.

After graduation, I worked the night shift in the hospital where I trained. The hospital had just opened a new critical care unit, only the second such unit in the State of Connecticut. It was a very new specialty in both medicine and nursing. Doctors and nurses were learning together as new technologies, medications, treatment modalities and equipment came flooding into our unit. I joined the pioneering staff and was the nurse in charge of the ICU on the night shift.

The nursing supervisor came by every night to get a report on the patients from me. Her name was Kit and she was funny and easy to talk to. However, she frequently brought the conversation around to homosexuality. I would always say something about how sinful it was. But, I was very attracted to her. She was what some might call butchy or masculine looking but I was intrigued by her looks and our age difference didn't matter to me, my age of twenty and Kit at forty.

I wanted to uphold the Christian teachings I grew up with but inwardly I was in turmoil, in love for the first time. I had protested weakly in our conversations about homosexuality. So one day, I decided to try to be a good Christian witness, a way of giving personal testimony about the goodness and salvation with God and Jesus and badness and hell of anything sinful.

I marked every verse in the Bible with anything to say about the sinful nature of homosexuality. After one of our night shifts, I took my Bible over to Kit's house and read her every passage I had marked. There were many, mostly in the Old Testament, as I remember, mixed in with other sins such as eating shrimp and lobster, having haughty eyes, and women speaking in the houses of God.

Kit listened. When I finished, I looked up at her. She stood up, walked over to where I was sitting, leaned down and kissed me. I closed my Bible.

That started five years of a roller-coaster life with conflicting emotions – the great joy of being who I really was, head-over-heels in love for the first time, the guilt of breaking off my engagement to Hector without telling him why, the frustration of waiting all those years for Kit to fulfill her promise to leave the woman with whom she was in relationship, the painful loss of all of my nursing school friends as rumors started surfacing about Kit and me, and the guilt for lying to my family about who Kit really was to me.

To cover the pain, I started drinking when I was not working. As a night supervisor, Kit had the keys to the pharmacy so she could get medications for the patients when the hospital pharmacy was closed. When alcohol became less effective in controlling my depression and anxiety over our relationship, Kit started getting medication to help me be "up" when I needed that and to help me sleep when I was exhausted. I was mixing alcohol with the various medications I got from her.

One night, after drinking several glasses of something alcoholic and taking some "uppers," I went over to Kit's house determined to force her to leave her partner. I didn't know how I was going to do that—I was drunk and high. I banged on her door and yelled for her to come out. Kit called the police and I was arrested for disturbing the peace. I spent the night in jail.

The next day, after a friend bailed me out, I decided I could not live that way anymore. There was nothing gay (happy) about the gay lifestyle. My experience had been mostly disappointment, pain and loss. The pain and loss of a love relationship promised but only dangled, of my self respect as I turned into a drinking, pill popping crazy woman. I no longer saw myself as a good, honorable daughter and sister. The pain and loss was all too great.

At the age of 25, with all the pills and alcohol I had left, I took an overdose. I don't remember wanting to kill myself, but rather, I did not want to hurt any more. My parents found me unconscious later that day, after I made a drunken call to my mother to ask if she had any more valium. I was taken to the hospital where I worked and it took me several days to fully wake up. While I was coming out of the coma, I was talking—talking about my life. It was the first time my parents and family were aware of my gay lifestyle. And the news of what I was saying about Kit and me verified the gossip already traveling the halls of the hospital, adding a scandalous layer and quickly spreading anew around the hospital.

After I recovered enough to go back to work, I was fired by the director of nurses for causing a scandal at the hospital. Kit was not fired. That perceived unfairness angered me for years. Some years later I was able to let that go though therapy.

The director, who was also gay and a friend of Kit's, said I needed to make a court appearance for the arrest but that Kit had dropped the charges. She said the judge would just let me go.

Since I was fired from my job, a very shameful experience for me, I decided to move someplace where I was not known. My brother lived in Long Beach, California. I arranged to drive there the next week. I wanted to figure out how to start my life over. I don't remember feeling much at all—maybe nothing. I was on auto-pilot, just doing the next thing in front of me, and that was to get out of town!

A few days after meeting with the nursing director, and still feeling emotionally off balance from the overdose, I went to court. My father went with me because I had never been in court before. I don't think he had either. In the courtroom, I found out that Kit had not dropped the charges. The judge called in a lawyer for me. I told the lawyer the whole sorry story, which he then relayed to the judge. When I told the judge I was planning to move to California the following week, he dropped the charges and said I was free to go.

Walking out of the courtroom with my father, he turned to me, anger in his eyes and said, "You make me sick!" He walked on, me following with my head hung low, my gut feeling like it had just been punched into my backbone.

Those four words reverberated through the next decades of my life. I was not conscious of that reverberation much of the time. Although my father knew about my lifestyle from the hospital and courtroom, my mother did not want me to say anything more to him about my being gay. She said she feared he would take his anger out on her, not physically, but in an angry tirade. So I never talked to him about my lifestyle, about that time in my life or about those words. Each time I visited my parents, it was as if that part of my life did not exist. My relationship with my father became superficial. After my mother died, 35 years later, I didn't call home for months at a time and rarely went back to Maine to visit him.

* * *

In summer of 2012, over forty years after the breach with my father, I was preparing for my second Camino walk. I wanted and needed to tackle the reason I was not connecting with my father. I knew I needed to forgive him for those words. He was 88 years old and I didn't know if he even remembered saying that sentence—I was pretty sure he did not remember.

That summer, as I walked the hills of Ashland, getting ready for my outer pilgrimage, I spent several weeks becoming an inner pilgrim. I worked through a process of forgiveness that had already helped me let go of a couple of other stubborn forgiveness issues in my life. I did not want Dad—or me, for that matter—to die with this un-forgiveness in my heart. I wanted to let it go for good.

Forgiveness is one of those inside jobs. If I am the one with un-Forgiveness in my heart, I am the only one who can fix it. It does not have anything to do with the other person. It does not matter if that person has really done something to me or not or whether I get an apology from that person or not.

I used the process of forgiveness outlined in a favorite book of mine by Linda Howe called *Healing Through the Akashic Records*. The process consists of getting to acceptance of what happened. That can be hard to do, but internally fighting against what has happened is not helpful to the self. I was able to get to acceptance.

Yes, I lived the life I had during my early twenties. Yes, I had been arrested. Yes, I had taken an overdose. Yes, I was gay. And Yes, Dad said those words to me.

Next in the process is being able to pardon the other. In Linda's concept of *pardon* it means we stop trying to extract some kind of compensation for what happened. We stop trying to get payback. Yes, after all those years, I could stop trying for any psychological payback from Dad.

A helpful concept of forgiveness in *Healing Through the Akashic Records* is to look at the probability of innocence. I thought about Dad in his early forties in 1970. There was very little understanding of gayness at that time and in our religion, it was a terrible sin. I thought about how he was raised and I understood that was the only way he could see my situation at the time. He had uncles, grandfathers and great grandfathers who were "hell and brimstone" preachers. If I were my father, would I have done better, given his upbringing and that time in our political and cultural under-standing of differences? I wasn't sure.

After moving through my own stubborn determination to hang on to those words, I was able to happily and completely forgive that forty-year-old man with 1970 religious and cul-tural beliefs and predispositions. I was also able to forgive my younger self for the choices I made, choices less than healthy and caring of my own self—the drinking and the drug-ging of a precious Soul.

* * *

As I was coming to completion with forgiveness of my father, I was walking eight to ten miles a day, four to five days a week, to ready for the Camino. During that sum-mer, several physical issues temporarily stopped me from walking, such as a stress fracture of my foot and a signifi-cant increase in my heart rate and breathing as a result of a small dose of thyroid medication. I stopped walking only long enough for whatever was happening to clear up, and then I was back to hiking up the back hills of Ashland.

Everything was arranged for a mid-September departure. I would take the plane to Madrid and a train and bus to Roncesvalles. At the top of the Pyrenees Mountains, I would meet my friends and start walking the Camino. A week before I was to leave, a pain started in my right leg—a kind of pain I had felt one other time in my life. The cause then was a blood clot in my left leg. This time, it was my right leg that was bluish, enlarged and very painful. I did NOT want to go to the hospital. I did NOT want to hear another diagnosis of blood clot. After a friend coerced me, I did end up in the emergency room and I did hear the diagnosis I dreaded, only this time there were several clots in my leg. How could that be? How could I have all of those blockages with as much walking as I was doing? No one knew for sure, but the end result was: no flying on a plane, and no walking the Camino. Damn!

A couple of weeks later, when I would have been on the Camino if the blood clots hadn't happened, Dad had a stroke. Almost immediately he started recovering some of his abilities. He spent a few weeks in rehab and was getting his mobility back but still had an inability to talk or swallow. He had a feeding tube put in and a few times I was able to speak with him on the phone, with his second wife conveying his response to me.

Then, he started losing ground. He became semi-conscious. My siblings and I flew home from various parts of the country. By then, my clotting issues were being treated and I was able to fly to Maine in time to spend about an hour alone with him. Having completed my forgiveness work around Dad, and with a clear and loving heart, I told him how much I loved him, how much I had learned from him and how happy I was to have had him as my father. It seemed like he was aware I was there. He died later that night. If I had walked the Camino, I would never have made it back in time. I might not have even known he was not doing well until after he died.

The day I arrived to see my dad was my 67th birthday. My great birthday present that year was spending those last hours with my father with a heart free from resentment and bitterness. My heart was happy for him. He had been a very active man his whole life, out in nature—farming, in the woods, on a lake, running a hunting and fishing lodge in the wilderness of Maine. He would have struggled in a body that could not function the way he wanted it to.

So Dad was able to move on and I was able to move on from resentment and pain to forgiveness. The process I went through to meet him with a clear, loving and open heart before his death set up a major healing for me.

A couple of months later, I would be at a place called the Monroe Institute, and see my father as a glorious Soul Being. The healing circle of Forgiveness was completed with an out-of-this-world conversation with Dad. That Healing helped launch me into my work as an Anam Aira, assisting the Healing of others across the Veil.

Chapter 4
A Lesson in Healing

"It is so wonderful to see you, Judy. We have things to talk about. I know you had a hard time with what I said to you those long years ago. I want you to know that you and I agreed, before coming into this life, that I would do something to you as a young adult that would be hard on you, but it would help you become a stronger person, able to speak and live from your true nature."
– Dad talking to me from the Other Side of the Veil

During my recovery time from the blood clots which kept me grounded from walking the Camino, the idea of learning to be an Anam Aira swirled around in my mind. It was about two and a half years since I first heard about Anam Aira from Richard. Maybe the desire to walk the Camino had gotten me off track from learning to escort people across the Veil at their moment of death—Veil meaning an energetic barrier between physical life and physical death. I thought the people who might benefit from that service would be those frightened of dying, who were hanging on to life much longer that anyone expected. They would be living out of a fear of dying, not because they were enjoying life. I knew hundreds of people like that in my career as a critical care nurse. Those were hard deaths to witness.

I believed I knew more about living and dying than what I knew as a critical care nurse. For over three decades, I had been reading Robert (Bob) Monroe's books, *Far Journeys and The Ultimate Journey*, over and over, wanting to encounter what he had as an Out-of-Body (OOB) practice. Bob was one of the first people to write about and explore Out-of-Body travel in the last half of the twentieth century. He didn't just travel locally—around places on Earth. He traveled to the Other Side of the Veil. His books described at least part of the territory over there.

Bob had hundreds if not thousands of experiences meeting Beings on the Other Side. He gained great wisdom as to how the Afterlife, indeed, all of Life, worked for the benefit of All. Bob eventually created an institute to teach others how to have those same kinds of experiences he had decades before as spontaneous events. He created a sound technology called Hemi-Synchronization. Listening to specifically embedded sounds on a CD helped people move into a deep meditative state and discover the levels of awareness Bob mapped as he explored the territory on the Other Side of the Veil.

I contemplated the possibility of attending the Monroe Institute in Virginia as a way to learn at least part of the process of escorting someone across the Veil. I saw two parts to the process of being an Anam Aira: the first was the ability to consciously connect to and be aware of when the person/ Soul was ready to leave their body. The second part was the process of escorting the Soul over—companioning the Soul to the Other Side where help was available—taking them to some "place" or dimension.

In becoming an Anam Aira, I knew that to escort people across the Veil at the moment of death I needed to know my way around on the Other Side, where to take each person as they crossed over. Going to the Monroe Institute was a way for me to learn about the different levels of awareness or "places" Bob described. I hoped I could acquire the skill to negotiate my way around the areas in the spiritual dimension.

Two months after my father died, I took my first Monroe program called "Gateway." It teaches the participants how to move to the Other Side of the Veil and to know and differentiate the various levels of expanded conscious awareness. I would learn which expanded awareness level the Soul needed to be taken to once I escorted them across the Veil.

My life detour brought me here. Canceling the Camino trip provided the money I needed to take three Monroe programs. And take them I did! A month after the Gateway program, I was at the Monroe Institute for two more, back to back.

In the "Lifeline" program I learned the process of escorting someone stuck in an *in between* environment on the Other Side to a Healing area where they could get help. I experienced many different levels of awareness in the spiritual domain. It was the second step in my plan to become an Anam Aira.

The next step was learning how to consciously connect to someone before they died, and to move across the Veil with them at the moment of death. But the Monroe Institute did not teach that part of the process. I thought that as I learned how to move around in the spiritual dimension, I might figure out that step. As it happened, I did just that.

Focus 27 is a level of awareness on the Other Side of the Veil separating physical life from what some call the Afterlife. It is a Way Station for some who have recently died where they heal, rest and recuperate, as well as being guided through a gentle Life Review. During one of my first trips to Focus 27, I had an amazing experience I had never thought possible.

Through a meditative process, I followed the Hemi-Sync sounds in my headset to the Park in Focus 27. Dad was there waving to me when I arrived! But he didn't look like his 88 year-old self who had died two months before. He seemed to be in his forties, fit and happy—vibrant even—shimmering. He had a big smile on his face and was waving Hi!

But where was I? Physically, I was in my CHEC unit (Controlled Holistic Environmental Chamber) at the Monroe Institute in Virginia, in an individual isolation booth. I lay on the bed with my headphones on. It was dark in my unit with no sound except what I heard through my headset from our facilitators in the control booth a floor below. I was consciously led by the sounds coming from a Monroe-designed CD, hoping to reach an expanded level of awareness Bob Monroe called Focus 27.

But the truth was, I was in my CHEC unit *and* in Focus 27, on the Other Side of the Veil, with my father. I was in two places at once. I learned later that I was in so many more than just two places. At this point, being at the Monroe Institute in Virginia and in the Park at Focus 27 at the same time was enough to deal with.

Dad was asking, *"Can we talk?"*

I enthusiastically answered, "Yes!" I was so happy to see him and wondered what he would say. In life, he was a man of few words. I didn't expect to see him on my first trip to this or any of the focus levels. I was a novice at this traveling-beyond-the-Veil process. I was surprised to see anything, but seeing my father topped all of my expectations.

I wondered if Dad was aware of the profound forgiveness process I was involved in a few months earlier. I didn't tell him about it when I sat at his bedside that last day as I told him how much I loved him.

Dad and I sat down on a beautifully carved bench in the dazzling Focus 27 Park. The Park was radiant with color—the trees a vivid mixture of various shades of green, many shades I had never seen before. There were patches of uniquely shaped and colored flowers positioned artistically around the Park.

A musical babbling brook flowed through the area, passing by the flowers and intricately carved benches where one could sit and take in all this beauty.

One of the biggest wonders of the place was the Light—a vibrant Golden Light that lit up everything and at the same time bathed everything in Presence—the amazing Existence of Life and Love Here.

Dad told me—or reminded me—that we agreed he would say something in our life on Earth to make me a much stronger person.

I answered him: "You are right, Dad. That was very hard at the time but it did help me over the years. At first, my thoughts about that time in our lives were always an angry "Fuck you, Dad." As the years passed, the 'fuck you' message became less about you and was for anyone who was trying to dominate or control me. I used that message until I didn't need to feel that aggressive response any more. I became a strong advocate for myself."

I told Dad about the process of forgiveness of our younger selves I experienced in the summer. I told him I was able to come to complete forgiveness of the whole situation a few months before he died and that I was able to be with him in love and gratitude that last afternoon. I asked him if he knew I was there that day.

Dad replied, "Yes, I knew you were there and I was so happy you had come to be with me. I knew in my soul why you had been distant from me after your mother died. I also knew the day you flew in to see me was your birthday and I didn't cross over until it was past midnight, for your sake.

"I know because you are still in a body it would be

helpful to have an apology from me. I do apologize for the pain I caused you. On this side, we know it was for the best, but I hurt you a great deal by those words and by my not acknowledging who you are in this life. I am sorry for that."

Those were wonderful words to hear from him. I felt nothing but love passing between us. Beautiful Golden Light surrounded us. It wrapped us in deep Love and Understanding.

It would take me at least a year to completely understand what Dad meant by "On this side, we know it is for the best...." As I traveled to the Other Side of the Veil many times over the next year or so, I learned that, as Souls, we choose the lessons we want to learn in a life. We are not victims. We deliberately set up the situations and circumstances that give us the best chance of encountering the lesson. We do this with the agreement of our Soul family. Every one participating in our life on Earth is a Soul who agreed to assist us in the lessons we chose. We do the same for each of them, to a greater or lesser degree.

Dad continued, "I'm so happy to see you and to see you Here. Would you like to see the place I have created Here?"

I had learned that in Focus 27 Souls are able to create their own unique place, a familiar environment in which to rest and recuperate after death. Focus 27 is a very creative environment. Just by thinking about the kind of place that would be comforting, that place is created.

This became a tool for me as I later discovered I could take people over there in the early process of dying so they could create their special place and have it waiting for them when they arrived after the final transition.

Dad and I zipped off to see the home he created for himself while he was in Focus 27. Travel in the Afterlife occurs immediately, just by intending to go somewhere or see someone.

Dad's special place was a combination of the sporting lodge he and my mother owned when I was in my late teens and early twenties, and the farm he grew up on in Northern Maine. It was beautiful with lots of animals and his horse from his youth, Blacky. The place was just perfect for Dad to recuperate.

When I connect with someone on the Other Side, it is at a Soul level, not at a personality level. From my experience with Dad's personality during my life, he would have been much less talkative and disclosing. I learned over time that when I meet someone in the Afterlife, they have gone through a Life Review and let go of all negative feelings about themselves or others. There is only Love and Gratitude left in the Soul.

After some time with Dad, I heard the sound cue on the CD, bringing me back to—to Here—to the Monroe Institute and my CHEC unit. There were tears rolling down my face from the unexpected and deeply healing experience. The better part of a lifetime of regret, anger and suffering was totally gone, and wondrous joy and love was in its place.

This was the first of many healings I have experienced over the years doing this work on the Other Side. I didn't know it at the time but, looking back, I see this healing with my father had to happen before I could assist others in their healing with Loved Ones across the Veil. My relationship with my father was completely healed with one of us on this side and one on the Other Side of the Veil—one living and one not living, at least not living in the way we think about living. It was a stunning example for me of what is possible. It would become my future work.

Chapter 5
Aspects of the Afterlife Territory

I was well-prepared for the work that led me to my connection with Dad. Over more than thirty years I read and re-read Bob Monroe's books, each time understanding a bit more about what he conveyed and the significance of the territories he defined on the Other Side of the Veil.

Monroe wrote about the difference between believing something and *Knowing* it. We know if a thing is true or not by experiencing it. Until that time, we are in a state of belief, not a state of *Knowing*. I was frustrated. I wanted to *know* what Bob knew but I was only in a state of belief because I had no experiences. I wanted to experience and, as Bob wrote many times in his books, turn a belief into a *known*. I wanted that *Knowing* very much and it briefly started at the Mount of Joy. Then the *Knowingness* was gone again.

In his early days of investigation, Bob Monroe described what was happening during his spontaneous "Out-of-Body" experiences. He noticed similarities in "places" or levels of awareness. He labeled them using the term Focus Levels as he assisted others so everyone had a common language.

The following information is paraphrased from the Monroe Institute website. It is a description of what Bob Monroe called Focus Levels of Awareness. I am including only the focus levels I discuss in *Soul Companion*. For a description of all the focus levels, see "Resources" on the Monroe Institute website: www.monroeinstitute.org.

C (consciousness) 1: The level of awareness in which most of us spend our normal, waking lives. It is the everyday, ordinary reality of the physical world in which we live.

Focus 23: In Focus 23, the Human inhabitants tend to be those no longer physically alive but have become "stuck" for some reason. Often, they are confused about or unaware of their physical death. Many in Focus 23 attempt to maintain contact with the physical world around familiar people or places. These we call ghosts. Focus 23 inhabitants are stuck because they are unable to move on through their own resources. The range of their free choices is extremely narrow. They are typically alone and completely isolated from communication with other Humans dead or alive. This can occur through the circumstances of their death or habitual patterns of thinking prior to death.

Focus 24, 25 and 26: Inhabitants of these levels are in what Monroe called The Belief System Territories. People are attracted to specific locations by Afterlife beliefs they held while physically alive. Every set of Afterlife beliefs held by Humans at any time in our history or future has a specific location within these focus levels. In a sense, The Belief System Territory inhabitants are stuck like those in Focus 23. The difference is they are not isolated from contact with others. All inhabitants of a specific Belief Territory are in contact with all others sharing their beliefs. Contact with anyone holding conflicting beliefs is severely limited. Free will choices here are restricted to only those compatible with the prevailing beliefs. Some of these areas look like Heavens, some look like Hells. Each one is rigidly structured around the beliefs held by the inhabitants. In Bob Monroe's experience, it is extremely difficult to move people from this area to areas of greater free will choice. In my more limited experience, if a Being *wants* to leave the Belief System they are in, they can be moved on quite easily. More about that later.

Focus 27: This is the Afterlife area with the greatest free will choice for its inhabitants. Before he spent more time exploring it, Monroe experienced Focus 27 as a beautiful park. It is an area created by Humans and often resembles physical Earth environments. Contact and communication is open between all inhabitants. Many residents living in Focus 27 provide assistance to new arrivals during their adjustments to living in the Afterlife. It is a highly organized and structured area. There are Centers of activity Here providing for their continuing development in the Afterlife. In Bob's experience, he found Centers for Education, Life Review, Rejuvenation, Planning, Scheduling, Rehabilitation, and many others. These Centers also coordinate activities in the physical world to assist in Human development on Earth.

According to Bob, Focuses 22 though 27 are Human thought-constructed areas, with Focus 27 giving the greatest opportunity for continued growth and development of the Being. As thinking and feeling Humans, we create the reality of our physical lives and to some degree, by those thoughts, the Afterlife in which we initially exist. Within a relatively narrow range of existence, we construct our lives, and the where and how we live those lives—in life after life and part of the between lives. Eventually, all parts of our Soul end up within our larger Soul Self.

My very first time in Focus 27:

I am in a most glorious Park. The whole area is surrounded by magnificent tall trees waving in the breeze, with vibrant green and multicolored leaves shimmering in the Light. The Light! The Light is a brilliant golden color coming from Everywhere in the Park and infusing everything. Flowers galore are interspersed between and around the trees. Flowers of every color, imaginable and not, every shape and incredibly fragrant. The grass is brilliant green and so soft on the bottoms of my feet – my feet? What does the rest of me look like? I can't tell – I see only my feet cushioned in the cozy thick grass.

As I look to my right, there is a brook flowing over crystalline stones – the stones and the water are effervescent with Energy and Joy. Joy and Love and Light and Presence are Here. The sounds of the running water and everything else contribute to the sounds of rapturous music. I am in Ecstasy.

As I look up from the brook, Dad and my deceased friends Louise, Pam and Bill walk toward me, each smiling, waving and radiating an openhearted welcome. They are iridescent – sparkling with Golden Light.

As my experience with my dad revealed, one of the ways to use one's creative abilities in Focus 27 is to craft one's own place—a home. It is a place to visit and to come to after one dies and goes through the recuperation period. I have created my most ideal place there—a wonderful cedar home on a bluff, overlooking the ocean. There is a place for my deceased horses – Ben, Prince, Princess, and Shasta; my dogs—Sophie, Kismet, Breezy and Nanook; and the many cats, rabbits and hamsters I have loved in my adult life. In this Afterlife setting I am able to converse with whales, dolphins and otters in the bay that extends beyond my home.

Are these animals really there? Yes, no, and of course. Yes, because I created a place for them and an intention for their essences to be close to me. And no, they are within their own Soul essences of Horse, Dog, Cat, Rabbit, Whale, etc. However, as Souls we all are in many places and in many forms at the same time—so, "of course."

During the Lifeline program at the Monroe Institute, we started our trips in Focus 27 and then moved to Focus 23 to find Beings who had died but needed assistance getting to where they could be helped. The idea of "moving" is more like changing one's area of focus. There may not be any sense of movement, rather more like looking in one direction and then shifting one's focus to another direction. Most of the time, my experience with changing my focus of awareness is that the results are instantaneous. As I enter Focus 27, after saying a person's name I am instantly with the person, wherever he or she is. At times, as I take people from Focus 23 to Focus 27, I do experience some sense of movement. It may be that since my attention is on the person I am taking with me, I slow down so I feel a sense of movement.

Beyond Focus 27: There are innumerable levels of awareness beyond Focus 27. These levels are beyond Human-thought construction. Almost all of what exists in the Afterlife is beyond Human thought-created areas. These are dimensions we have no control over and they are glorious beyond our imagination. I will highlight some of my experiences beyond Focus 27 in the chapters to come. They also require a much greater expansion of consciousness to navigate and communicate.

* * *

I didn't have the *Knowingness* most of my life but I have read many authors who wrote about the Afterlife. One such author whose work has been very helpful in my initial understanding of the Afterlife is William Buhlman. In William's exploration of the Other Side, he investigated many of the same areas Bob called the Focus levels. William is a teacher and guide for others in exploring the area beyond the Veil. He began having what he called self-initiated Out-of-Body experiences in 1972. He has written many books about his experiences, including: *Adventures Beyond the Body, The Secret of the Soul, Adventures in the Afterlife* and *Beyond the Astral*. As with Bob Monroe, William Buhlman experienced his explorations as

"leaving the body"—raising above it or out of it—and continuing on to have life-altering experiences. William, like Bob
Monroe, became aware of what was happening to him in a
deeper way as he experienced that travel. He understood
he was not going "out of his body," but going inward. It is an
inward journey, into the core of himself and the Universe—
not an outward journey.

William describes the experience of moving beyond this
physical level of a physical body. His understanding is that,
as Souls, we occupy all levels of awareness or dimensions
at the same time. Therefore, how we experience places and
situations is a matter of where our attention is focused.
According to William, we have the ability to experience vast
levels of awareness but, after physical death many people
initially only experience areas close to the physical plane
because that is where their focus continues to reside.

The idea of a second body or astral body is consistent
with descriptions of the auric field of a physical/spiritual
body. According to Barbara Brennan, the author of *Hands of
Light: A Guide to Healing Through the Human Energy Field*,
our energy field surrounds the physical body. It has seven
layers. The first three layers closest to the body are related
to the physical plane and the physical body. The next layer,
moving out about a foot from the body, is the astral level. It
is the bridge between the inner layers of the physical plane
and the outer three layers associated with the spiritual
plane. As Brennan describes the astral level of the energy
field, it is more amorphous and not shaped as distinctly as
the physical body. It makes sense that we would move into
the astral body as we traverse the Focus Levels closest to
the Earth.

What Monroe called the Human thought-constructed areas
of Focus 22 to 27, Buhlman refers to as "consensus reality."
All of the people occupying a particular level of awareness

have the same beliefs about what exists there. Those beliefs come from what each of those people, before death, believed would happen to them after they died. When they die, they experience exactly what they believed they would experience.

William describes the different realities as having a particular vibrational or frequency level. Everyone resonating at a similar frequency will inhabit the same consensus reality or beyond. William differentiated the realities based on the degree of conscious awareness a person developed in this life and the Afterlife.

Some people are psychologically stuck in their physical life on Earth—not knowing what to do to get their life back on track. If they die while feeling stuck in life, they may not even be aware they have physically died. They find themselves in the same situation, the same environment, and will try to interact with the life they no longer have. For example, on the Other Side of the Veil I once found a teenager in what seemed like an art room. I discovered later that he shot himself in his bedroom—where he did many creative projects. If the people who are stuck in the Afterlife are willing to accept help, I, or others like me, can move them to another focus level where there are Guides to help them.

More on this later. Every trip crossing the Veil has been satisfying to me, but to move someone who is stuck is deeply rewarding to them because they can continue their journey to wholeness as a Soul.

* * *

B ack to the Park: *As I see Dad, Louise, Pam and Bill, all who had died months to years earlier, I am joyous. Both Dad and Bill tell me they will talk to me later and move on. I am now standing with my long time friend, Louise, who died about four years earlier, and Pam, another dear friend who died about 6 months earlier.*

I introduced Pam and Louise years before. They became great friends in the years Louise battled metastatic breast cancer and Pam was ending her long career as director of a well-regarded school of nursing. Pam was with Louise in the hours before Louise died. During that visit Pam created a deeply loving ceremony by honoring Louise's life with a champagne toast. Louise, with a big smile, had her champagne on a fresh mouth swab.

I spend a Joyful while with Pam and Louise, laughing and reminiscing. Both tell me about their wondrous experiences but mostly, we are just together, being in each other's Presence. Perfection!

Chapter 6
Awakening – Again

Ilove exploring new territory. Until I went to the Monroe Institute, that territory was where I could touch the ground—walk on the Earth. However, during my third residential program at the Monroe Institute, our facilitators gave us a chance to explore in detail the expanded level of awareness called Focus 27. I looked forward to spending extended time there. We understood there was much to explore.

As I meandered around in non-physical existence, I found myself in a very large, ornate stone structure known as The Library. It seemed solid and yet not. I understood later that this Library is an area or specific level of awareness where one has access to all information, knowledge and wisdom of the Universe. In this place of knowledge, I looked around and wondered what to do or what question to ask. I saw no books, but I was aware that if I wanted a specific book, it would appear. I *knew* that if I had a question of any kind, it would immediately be answered. But, what question did I have?

Suddenly I saw the entire back of The Library open to reveal the expansiveness of the whole Universe—waiting for me! I saw my feet at the very edge of The Library floor and—well, Space. Like pictures taken by the Hubble telescope, *that* Space—only incredibly more vivid. My barefoot toes were just over the edge of what seemed like solid flooring. Beyond my toes was open Space, with stars and galaxies, brilliant colors of dust and gases, with no end in sight. The thought came to me, *"No boundaries, no beginnings, no endings, just Being."* Me, exploring the likes of which I never thought possible but had always wanted!

As I experienced Being out in the Universe, I wrote an inadequate description. There are very few words in the paragraph below. Could every word take in the Wholeness of This? There are *no* words I know of that could possibly describe this except "ineffable." Trying to capture the experience, I wrote this at the time:

> *I step out into the vast Universe. The experience of profound Wisdom, the spectacular Beauty, the Presence of the Universe. The Aliveness of Everything. The Peace, the overwhelming Love of the Universe. To be out There – just floating – just Being – experiencing the immensity of the Presence of All – All Light – All Love – All Understanding – All Compassion – All Experience – Everything – Timeless – All There Is....*

After eons of time, I heard our facilitators calling us back to normal consciousness through the headsets. It took me hours to really come back from that experience, and though it happened years ago, I'm not sure I am still back to who I was before.

And Time—what to say about "How long did it last?" I know that each of our Hemi-Sync CDs lasts about 45 minutes, but to me it felt like an eternity. Eternity and Infinity. Two words that might capture the enormity, the profoundness of this experience, but I don't think so.

As I thought about this later, I could not tell if I had been in the real physical Universe or in some aspect of the expansiveness on the Other Side of the Veil. Years later when I asked my Guides who had made themselves known to me over time, the answer was: both and more. They wanted to give me a profound experience and they knew I loved astronomy. They wanted me to relate both to something known—like our physical Universe—*and* experience dimensions unknown to me.

I now understand that nothing experienced on the Other Side of this Life can be described in just two possible answers—it is not just either/or, yes/no, here/there or This Side/Other Side of the Veil. There is no dualism. There are an infinite number of "correct" answers, depending on what a Being can comprehend in awareness.

We exist in all dimensions; beyond Time and Space and within Time and Space—multidimensional—at the same time. The totality of our consciousness is infinite. We are generally only aware of the here and now of Earth. Yes, we are here and now and on Earth. And we are also on the Other Side of the Veil. We are having lifetime after lifetime after lifetime—at the same time—from the perspective of the Other Side of the Veil—from the perspective of Eternity. There is no concept of time once we leave our physical life. There is only the Eternal Now.

No past. No future. Just Now. No form. Just Being. No thoughts. Just experiencing. No feelings. Just Love. Incredible Light and Joy and Peace and Love beyond description.

While at the Monroe Institute, after each episode of listening to a Hemi-sync CD and having our experiences, we gathered as a group and debriefed with our facilitators. After my encounter with the Universe—the incredible *Knowing* of the Presence of Light—I opened my mouth to say what happened to me and no words came out. I was in a state of Ecstasy, with no verbal or non-verbal skill to express what my whole Being was still vibrating from and with. After a time, our facilitators said I might be able to articulate the experience better as it sank into my Being. The truth is I can't articulate the encounter any better now than at the time it happened.

As I continued to access the Other Side of the Veil, I now know answers to questions people ask me about the Other Side. I am frequently as surprised by my answers as the person asking the questions. I am not aware of knowing that answer before the question is asked. I don't think about the answer, it just comes as I open my month to speak. Normally, I ponder questions before answering, but these answers come immediately.

* * *

Back home, and many months later, I unexpectedly connected with the person, the Being, who facilitated my boundless experience in the Universe. In physical life, Kathleen was a high school pal of my friend, Theresa. Theresa asked me to check on Kathleen because she heard she had died of cancer.

I found Kathleen to be a joyous facilitator of the gifts of The Library in a remarkably expansive level of awareness. This role allowed her to support this glorious function for all Creation to access. Kathleen came to this expansive awareness level after she passed over the Veil. It was a focus of awareness where much could be done and learned by those who transition from life on Earth to this place.

Kathleen loved this place, this function, this offering of the Universe. She had been here many, many times—as seeker, as student, as teacher, and now—*now*—as a facilitator of that function. This calling had long been in her Being but she needed to be taught; guided by the masters before she could take her place among them.

The Library's function and place in the Universe is ancient and available for those who require or desire information and wisdom or access to records – personal, group, societal or universal. The Library has been known by many names through the ages, such as the Book of Life or the Akashic Record. It is an area where Masters and Guides assist with great growth and development for the Beings there. There is a transparency of thought, under-standing and intent inherit in this expanded awareness setting.

The Library is a very large golden-colored stone build-ing, shaped in the style of an ancient cathedral, with tall interior pillars reaching to the ceiling several stories above. The pillars line both sides of a long, wide central walk-way traversing the entire length of the building. There are small alcoves along the length of The Library where groups meet to learn from Masters, Guides or others.

While at the Monroe Institute, I learned that people experi-ence The Library differently. I think it is the lens or personal experience each person brings to this place. Some see it as an education center while others experience it as a library. I saw it as a library, with characteristics of my beloved Chartres Cathedral.

Kathleen guides explorers to the energy in The Library to access the knowledge they seek. She facilitates all of this through her energy field, her Source of Being, the purity of her Love and Compassion. Many others join her in this sacred role. She can imagine no greater honor, no greater service to all Beings and all Creation than the role she has been given.

I was acutely aware that Kathleen facilitated my profound experience where The Library opened up, allowing me to float out into the Universe. The awareness, the utter *Knowingness* of her part in my experience was absolute.

With this role, Kathleen has access to all that is within The Library – such a depth of understanding is present

Here to All There Is. Profound – Simple – Ecstatic –
Humbling – Jubilant – Stillness – Love – Yes – Yes – Yes.

Years later, as I wrote the first draft of this chapter, I was stunned by a revelation. My connection with The Library in Focus 27 and the experience of floating out into the Universe was a reconnection with the *Knowingness* I thought I lost after the Camino in 1997. What an overpowering insight it was as I sat back in my chair and thought, 'Wow! Wow!" I was dumbfounded. And then profoundly grateful to Kathleen and the Guides of The Library for thc return of what I had longed for!

That *Knowingness* has been re-infused with a sense of depth and breadth of All There Is. My spiritual guide, Gangaji was right—IT had not left me, only my awareness of IT had changed. That awareness has come back with great joy! With assistance from Beings from the Other Side, a re-awaking in me occurred. A couple of very important dots were connected from my Heart and Soul—across Time and Space.

Chapter 7
No Longer Alone and Empty

While attending The Monroe Institute's Lifeline program, I began each session by grounding myself in Focus 27. After moving into a meditative state, I went to the deck of my cedar home I created in Focus 27 a few days earlier. I set the intention of finding someone caught in Focus 23 who needed assistance. Focus 23 is the label Bob Monroe gave to the area where people were trapped after death in a mind-loop of thinking preventing them from moving on in the Afterlife.

My focus of awareness shifted between my cedar house in Focus 27 and Focus 23, where those trapped could be found. I was aware I was near the territory Bob called The Belief System Territory, Focus 24–26, the focus levels where people reside if they held specific and strong beliefs about their experience in the Afterlife. If a person had a more open concept of the expansive possibilities after death, they generally move beyond the Belief Systems to Focus 27 upon leaving their body. There are much greater opportunities for growth of the Soul in Focus 27 than in the Belief Systems. In the Belief System, they experience just what they believe they will.

While learning to retrieve people from Focus 23, I didn't want to go to the Belief System areas, concerned that the Beliefs I had as a child and young adult might trap me. That is not possible and I suspect that our facilitators told us we would not get trapped, but I did not remember that initially. I made up a story in my mind that I might get stuck. The truth is, if I want to move out of a situation on the Other Side of the Veil, all I need to do is open my eyes and I am immediately back in regular consciousness.

One day, as I shifted my attention from my cedar deck in Focus 27 to Focus 23, I felt a pull to the Belief System Territory. While I learned this process at the Monroe Institute, my experience was one of cruising over the top of the Belief System as I moved from Focus 27 to 23. I still start out in Focus 27 but as I think about the person I am going to find, I am immediately with them, with no sense of travel.

But this time, I felt a magnetic tug pulling me toward the Belief System as I traveled toward Focus 23. I determined I would not be diverted to the Belief System and resolutely went on to Focus 23, on a Mission to find more people who needed help. When I arrived, there was no one there. That never happened to me before. There were always people waiting for help—but not this time.

I was not sure what to do. I wondered if I was being called to the Belief System. I had enough trust in the process that even with my concern of being trapped, I reluctantly shifted back there. Hovering over the area, I felt the pull again and this time, I allowed myself be taken down.

I am in a nun's cell – in the medieval time when nuns live in small stone rooms in a convent, or the crypt of a church. This room is bare of furniture with only a small bed, a table for a candle and a single wooden chair. There is a nun pacing around her small room, repeating over and over to herself, "I need to be freed from here. I don't believe these teachings any more." Her name is Sister Mary.

I talked to Sister Mary, saying I could help her move to a better place. There was a pillar behind me in the corner of the room. (The ability to "see" or be aware of all directions simultaneously exists on the Other Side.) There were several other nuns sticking their heads out from behind the pillar. I thought they did not want to be seen but were interested in our conversation. I didn't pay much attention to them, as I was focused on convincing Sister Mary I could help her leave that place. I explained:

"Sister Mary, I can take you to a place where you will have much more freedom – freedom of thought and wondrous possibilities for expanded learning, if you would like."

"Yes, yes, I need to get out of this restricted area. I don't fit here any more. Please help me," Sister Mary replies, with a visible sense of relief.

I lift off, holding Sister Mary's hand. As we begin to rise, a nun runs out from behind the pillar and grabs Sister Mary's other hand, and then another nun grabs that nun's hand, until there are six or seven nuns in a row, each holding onto the hand of the nun in front of her.

As I see it now in my mind's eye, it reminds me of the scene in *Peter Pan*, one child holding on to Peter's hand and each of the others holding onto the hand of the child in front of them, so there is a stream of people lifting off to fly away.

As we land in the Park in Focus 27, I step down first and move to the side of where Mary will touch down so I can see her from a side view. Sister Mary steps down onto the landing area. Then, the next nun lands – and moves into the back of Mary – becomes integrated into Mary. Each nun does that – entering into the back of Sister Mary after landing, until all have landed and only Sister Mary is there. She is facing my Guide, Samantha, who is always waiting when I retrieve someone and bring him or her to Focus 27. Usually Samantha then takes the person I have retrieved to wherever is appropriate for that person.

But this time, my Guide does not take Sister Mary anywhere. Sister Mary turns to me, walks toward me until she is right in front of me. She turns around and backs into me – integrates into me! I feel – wow – I feel complete – even though I am not aware of feeling incomplete just a second earlier. I stand there with tears coming down my whole Being. I am complete. I don't know how to explain what that means to me – only those words describe the sensation. I am rooted there for some time – or no time – or all Time. I am not empty – I am not alone. I am complete. I am ecstatically Joyful.

The experience slowly fades and I am left—complete and deeply moved, tears rolling down my face, into my ears and onto the pillow my head is lying on in my isolation unit at the Monroe Institute.

When the energy of Sister Mary and all the other nuns came into me that day, it gave me the sense of completeness I had not felt for seventeen years, not since that time on the Camino, at the Mount of Joy. Weeks later when the awareness of how the Universe worked had gone, I'd also felt empty and alone. In the ensuing years after the Camino, I became used to that background feeling of emptiness and it was my norm. I was now integrated with a feeling of wholeness I had briefly experienced seventeen years earlier. I still feel that completeness every day.

I have one bit of information to add to the story of Sister Mary and the rest of the nuns. For more than thirty years, when I first meet people, many of them think I am or have been a nun in this lifetime. Two of my friends told me that their inclination upon seeing me is to call me Mary or Sister Mary. I didn't understand that before Sister Mary entered me. I still don't totally understand how the "nun" energy was in me before all of the nuns entered me that day. Perhaps something to do with Past Lives. I do feel and know that the Sister Mary energy internally completes me in this lifetime.

* * *

Later that week at the Lifeline program, I retrieved another important Soul who also impacted me personally—a little girl from a church in the South of France. She was about three years old. She wore a long white dress and had light golden hair. As she wandered inside a burned-out church I *knew* she was trying to find her parents. I understood that she was of the Cathar religion.

The Cathars were a religious sect active between the 12th and 13th centuries in Southern France and Northern Italy. Also known as the "pure ones" or the sect of the Good Men or Good Christians, they lived simple lives with few possessions. They were taught by ascetic priests who had few guidelines for worship, unlike the Catholic Church of the time. The Catholic Church denounced the sect because they did not follow the Catholic practices or venerate the Pope.

Pope Innocent III tried to bring the sect into compliance with the Church. He was not successful and launched the Albigensian Crusade in 1203 to wipe them out. One of the practices of the crusading knights was to round up a group of Cathers, lock them in a church and set it on fire. All those inside burned to death.

I knew about the history of the Cathars and that Crusade because I visited the hilltop château of Montsegur in the South of France years earlier. Montsegur was the last stronghold of Cathar resistance against the crusaders and the Catholic

Church. The final remaining "pure ones" walked down the hill empty handed after they ran out of food and water and were burned to death in a huge bonfire at the foot of the hill. That ended the Albigensian Crusade – and the Cathars.

When I walked down from the hilltop at Montsegur, I could almost feel the heat of the fire—a fire that had done its terrible damage and burned out centuries ago. There is a marker at the site of the bonfire. With my lifelong fear of being burned to death, I had a difficult time even looking at the marker.

Later, at the Monroe Institute, when I found the little girl in the church, I *knew* how and why she died. I understood all the other Cathars in the church moved to the Other Side of the Veil as they died. The little girl had not and was left trying to find her parents. Because there is no Time on the Other Side of physical life, the little girl did not know that many centuries had passed since she, her parents and the other Cathars had died.

With a feeling of compassion, I picked her up in my arms, cuddled her and took her to Focus 27. My Guide, Samantha, was there to meet us. I thought I might hand the little girl to her and she would take her to an appropriate place, as usual. But instead, Samantha escorted me, as I carried the little girl in my arms, to my special home on the bluff. As we walked up to my place in Focus 27 there was a small stone house in the yard I had not put there. It was the kind of stone house common in the Middle Ages, a house the young girl might find comforting. I opened the door to find a large soft, cozy bed that took up almost the whole Space. I laid the little girl in the bed and lovingly tucked her in. I went back to my work of retrieving others, as the Hemi-Sync CD directed me.

The little girl was a form of me from that lifetime and she needed to be comforted by my Soul's energy for some time before moving on. When I went back to my place later that evening, the small house was gone and so was the little girl. She was on her way, back to our larger Soul Self. Years later, I will see her and all of the Sister Mary nuns again.

It was another profoundly healing experience, another sense of integration. When I found the little girl in that church, I was very aware of my fear of being burned to death. I had been petrified of it my whole life.

Early in my career as a critical care nurse, I took care of several seriously or critically burned people. I saw the tremendous impact of fire on their bodies, their emotions, their thoughts about themselves and on their lives. I was very uncomfortable around those poor patients. I had no words of encouragement. I had nightmares for days or weeks after taking care of a burn patient. Now, that fear no longer exists. It dissipated the day I found the little girl and took her to my place.

And I am no longer alone—nor is Sister Mary, the other nuns or the little girl from the burned out church. More dots connected for me and my Soul.

Chapter 8
No Longer Afraid

I am delightfully surprised I have had no reaction to the anger I experience from those stuck on the Other Side. I am not afraid, or in any way put off by their behavior. In the presence of the anger, I feel totally calm and focus only on my reason for being there—to help the person move on to a place where they are no longer alone. They are coming Home—to belonging, to inclusion. The best Home any one of us on Earth could ever imagine.

As a child, I was very afraid of my father's anger. I would freeze, unable to think. I remember many times when he asked me to get a particular tool from the garage when he was working on some piece of equipment. If I could not find it immediately, Dad yelled at me to hurry up. When he raised his voice, I could never find the tool, even though he came stomping over and picked up exactly what he wanted. It was frequently right in front of me.

Fear of anger continued to haunt me throughout my early adulthood. As a young nurse, I felt like cowering and sometimes I did as an angry doctor yelled at me for some reason. Or no reason. But over time and with therapy, I developed a greater sense of self.

If I needed to be a patient advocate, I could stand up to the anger with all my strength—to doctors, a supervisor or a CEO. But it took overriding my fear to do that—my sense of advocacy was stronger than my fear.

The following encounter was just the opposite. It was a different and yet profound experience in retrieving a trapped Soul for Lisa, a client of mine three years after starting the Anam Aira work. This is another example of connecting with a dead Loved One who was in that mind-loop and believing he was still in his previous life.

Lisa asked me to see if I could connect with her father. She experienced physical and emotional abuse from him as a child. The emotional abuse continued into her adult life and she still felt somehow tied to him, even though he died many years ago. She felt bound by some force she could not explain, trapped and unable to more forward in her life.

I went to the Other Side to find Lisa's father, Stephen, in the same way I did at the Monroe Institute. I put on the hemi-sync CD, moved into a meditative state, moved to Focus 27 and called Stephen's name.

Stephen, in a loud and bellowing voice, "Yes. Who are you?"

I reply, "Hi Stephen. My name is Judy. Your daughter, Lisa, wanted me to check on you."

Stephen, loudly and angrily, "Who is she to ask you to do that? What does she want from me now?"

I now start to see Stephen. He is in an empty court-room. His response to me echoes through the cavernous room. There are papers all over the floor and desks. He paces back and forth in front of an empty jury box, making a case to the jury. But he is not saying anything and there is no one else in the room. He is wildly gesturing but not speaking – at least not out loud.

On the table where his papers are haphazardly stacked, there are also several empty shot glasses lined up. After a period of time of gesturing and pacing in front of the jury box, he comes back to the table and grabs a glass to take a drink. There is nothing in any of the glasses.

He growls at the empty glasses, and then goes back to the jury box.

I have connected with many people on the Other Side stuck in a mind-loop much like Stephen. I frequently find the person in an environment consistent with an important aspect of his or her life. The person is trying to interact with their old life but there are no other people in the space. Nothing they do to connect with that life works. The person is alone and stressed. The situation varies, but there is a consistent pattern of loneliness and fear, no matter how they act.

Stephen repeats this sequence again and again. It is at this point he acknowledges seeing and hearing me. He looks up – shocked to see me.

Stephen yells – his voice reverberates off the walls. "What are you doing in here? You're interrupting this trial!"

I calmly answer, "I am here to help you, if you would like."

Stephen, immediately reacting with a bellowing voice, "I would NOT like!"

Stephen goes back to his gesturing in front of the jury box – mouthing but not saying any words. He occasionally glances up at me and then goes back to the same routine – pacing in front of the empty jury box and trying to drink from an empty glass on the table.

After a time, he stops, faces me and yells, "What are you doing here? You are interrupting a whole trial. Get out of here!"

I again respond with, "I am here to help you, if you would wish that."

If I continue to repeat why I am there and don't add any information that could complicate the situation, the people I work with will almost always come around and allow me to help. I need to move them out of the environment they imagine themselves in and I cannot do that without their permission.

Stephen comes back at me. "God damn it – you are interrupting everything!"

As we face each other, Stephen shaking with anger, the courtroom starts to disappear. It slowly fades away. We are now in an empty room – gray cement on all sides, including the floor and the ceiling.

Stephen starts to cry. He falls to the floor, crying – sobbing – pounding his fists on the cement floor.

I say to Stephen, "I can take you to a place where you will be loved and helped, if you would like."

Stephen, looking up between sobs, "Yes – yes."

There is one thing I need to ask Stephen to do before taking him to Focus 27. I say, with a voice of authority, "Before we go, you need to release all of the psychic bonds you created in this past lifetime to bind your family. Will you do that?"

The only times I am aware of restraining ties between a person who died and someone still living is when the deceased is stuck between this world and where they can get help. Each time I have noted a bond, I ask the deceased to release it before I move them on. I have the sense, but am not completely sure, that release would happen automatically as they move through the healing process in Focus 27. But it does seem the healing process begins when the unhealed person is willing to break the bond that has bound another while in the same unhealed state as when they created it. I want to make sure the bond is eliminated so I request it be broken.

Stephen, still sobbing – saying these words between sobs, "Yes – Oh – Yes."

I am immediately aware he has broken the bonds and say, "Okay, Stephen, hold my hand and we will go."

I take Stephen to the Park in Focus 27. There are many people there who know and love Stephen, the Soul Essence of Stephen. He is lovingly welcomed back Home – hugs – gently holding him as he slowly stops sobbing.

As he stands in their midst, he is like a gentle little boy. He is a young, innocent, loving Being. After some time, his Loved Ones lead Stephen to the Healing Center. He will be well-loved and taken care of there.

Stephen was no longer alone, angry, and frightened. He was at the beginning of coming Home. In the Healing Center, Stephen will have the debris of the previous lifetime cleared away. Later, Stephen will work with his Guides as they lead him through a loving and supportive Life Review. He will then work on the lessons he missed in this last life. But for now, he is wrapped in the arms of love.

I read this experience to Lisa. She immediately felt freed. She *was* freed. The connection I had with her father and the request to disconnect any bonds he had over his family completely severed any restrictive ties Lisa felt from her father.

During many connections I have with people who are stuck, I experience the emotional state of the person as either afraid or angry. I do believe that fear is hidden by those who present with anger. I think it is a reaction to hiding the fear from self and others and trying to still have control over it.

Those who present as afraid come with me easily and I can take them to a place where they can be helped and loved. They have very little resistance to being helped and are grateful for it.

But this experience of being totally calm in the presence of angry, stuck people is different. I have no sense of trying to control my fear of the outburst. I have no reaction—yes, *no* reaction to the anger. I truly have no fear to overcome. My core is calm. My only mission is to help. The absence of fear, now on this side as well as the Other Side of the Veil, continues to be one of those transformative miracles created by following this guided path as a Soul Companion.

Those who are angry initially resist any help and act like they are in total control. They tend to yell and try to intimidate me. I stay calm in the midst of whatever behavior they show. At some point, the person deflates—as if they have puffed themselves up to seem menacing. By the time I take the person to Focus 27, each person has become like a little innocent child—no anger, only the purity of the Soul Essence.

I began this path of Anam Aira at the Sacred Art of Living Center by learning that the concept of Anam Aira existed. That was an unforgettable wake-up call to me. Arriving at the Monroe Institute to learn how to cross to the Other Side was an incredible time of learning who we really are as Souls. My ongoing practice of this skill and art continues to teach me that none of us are really alone. All fear dissolves as we learn who we actually are—eternal, vibrant, free and loving Souls.

Chapter 9
Discovering and Trusting The Work

For the first year and a half of being an Anam Aira, the work was incredibly engaging. I had no major worries about what I was doing. I was almost always surprised and sometimes even stunned by what I got as I went over to the Other Side to connect with people whose Loved Ones on this side of the Veil asked me to find.

I moved into a meditative state and said the person's name. Immediately I was with that person. The information came to me visually as "a scene" that I saw in my mind and/or a *Knowing* of what to write and what the person was *saying*. I did not hear a voice in my head or, more dramatically, voices external to me. It was and still is more subtle than that. But any time I have tried to put words down that I didn't initially *feel*—if I tried to consciously put my own words down for clearer understanding—I got a "No" and the flow would stop until I learned to write only from the flow of *knowing*. There was a flow of *Knowing* until the scene faded or the *Knowing* stopped. That's when the interaction was over.

I felt a little doubt begin to creep into my awareness, but I felt like that was a good thing. I thought it would keep me humble.

I welcomed the little twinge of uncertainty, that little wave of doubt softly traversing my mind. Was this really happening?

I didn't want to feel egotistical about this amazing ability I discovered within me.

Many people who asked me to connect with their Loved Ones on the Other Side came away with a healing of their own psychological wounds that occurred in physical life with that person. If there were unresolved conflict or struggle within the relationship with the transitioned person while they were both in body, there was frequently a residue left for the person still alive. It may even be more pronounced for the survivor, as most people believe they have lost all chance to heal the situation. They might be in turmoil as to what to do with the sorrow, regret, anger, jealousy or even hatred.

As for the person I connect with on the Other Side, they are most often in one of two states. If the person has recently crossed over they may be in an expanded state of awareness and working on uncompleted lessons from the life just finished, maybe learning additional skills.

If I find the person in such an awareness level, they may be in the middle of, or have completed, a guided Life Review. This is guided by Beings on the Other Side who have known that person for eons. My experience with many people is that this Life Review takes more integration time than the rapid Life Review described by those who have a Near Death Experience. During this process, the transitioned person looks at their life and focuses on accepting full responsibility for any conflicts, struggles or pain in relationships during that life. They let go of blame, judgment, anger, bitterness, hatred and guilt; any emotion that takes the focus away from their responsibility in the situation.

We might expect that taking responsibility for actions in life causes the person a sense of guilt or regret. It does not. The view from that side is an expansive one. One can see the broader lessons as well as the agreements made before coming into that life. We can see that lessons and agreements benefit one or both individuals. And importantly, they were agreed upon by both Souls. Seeing situations from the broader view, the transitioned person understands and accepts those lessons as part of the process of living a physical life. No guilt, regret or remorse is appropriate at that level, only a deep understanding of the process and events. If a person is inclined to take on those negative feelings, loving Guides help the individual reach the healthy perspective—responsibility and accountability for one's life lessons without guilt.

The emphasis here is that these matters affect both sides of the Veil. When I saw my father in Focus 27, two months after he died, Dad remembered what he said to me 45 years earlier causing me great pain most of my life. He knew it would be helpful to me to have an apology and he did apologize for the pain he caused. He also reminded me that we both agreed he would do something that would initially hurt me but be helpful in the long term. From that broader prospective, we both took responsibility for our part of the agreement. It was a very healing moment for me. It completely eliminated the resentment of him I had hung on to for forty-four years.

Most people transition easily but some get stuck in Focus 23. If the person was emotionally and mentally stuck in their life before death, they may be in that same unresolved situation after death. There can be a continuous loop of thinking/feeling that lasts into the Afterlife. They frequently do not know they are physically dead and blame others for the situation in which they find themselves.

If the person I find is in that mind-loop, they may be holding onto the same emotions and judgments they had in life. I am able to move them to a place where they will have time in the Healing Center. Then, they can complete the process of Life Review with help from gentle Guides.

What follows is a description of finding three people from the same family. The healing was for each of those who had died *and* the one member of the family still alive and in extraordinary pain.

Barbara called to talk with me after I began connecting with deceased members of families. She was interested in the stories where healing occurred for those still alive. She grew up in a very dysfunctional family. Except for her loving father who died decades earlier, Barbara's experience of family was devoid of the happiness, love and mutual support she witnessed in other families she knew. She spent most of her life trying to fix the dysfunction in the family. When she realized fixing was not possible, her strategy turned to distancing herself from her family of origin.

In the years before my involvement, Barbara's mother, Jean, died. Barbara's older brother, Jason, died a year after his mother. The last sibling, Brad, took his life the year before Barbara asked for my help. None of the three siblings had children. Therefore, Barbara was the last living person of that family. After her brother's suicide, she felt particularly disquieted in relationship to her family and the memories of the dysfunction.

Neither Barbara nor I knew what to expect in this session. But she knew she wanted relief from the despair. Left with painful, unresolved issues with each family member, she didn't know how to come to peace with the effects of the family dysfunction.

She asked if I could find her mother and her two brothers. She said if I came upon her father who died decades earlier, that would be great. But she was worried about the others, not her father. She experienced him as the only one with the capacity to love and care about her and the rest of the family.

I had not gone to find multiple people before and was unsure if I could do it. Would I be able to find and connect with each person? This was one of many requests I have received over the years asking me to do something I have not done before. My response to such requests is always, "I don't know if I can do that, but I will give it a try."

I found each of the three deceased members of Barbara's family. Each one was caught in the mind/emotion loop, each in their own unique situation. I first found Barbara's mother, Jean, as she was the person who had died after Barbara's father.

Jean sits in a stuffed living room chair. She has her hands folded but cannot move them. She can't get out of the chair. She leans forward to try to stand up but she can't move her arms, hands or legs. She is stuck in the chair. She is in a rage, yelling, "God damn it, get me out of here. What have they done to me? Why are they keeping me prisoner here? It's all their fault. Damn it, get me out of here."

She believes people she knows have wished her here and are holding her prisoner in the chair.

I watch Jean in the chair for a few minutes. I am outside of the scene, as if looking through a one-way mirror into the room. Then I enter the room where she struggles. Her expression shows surprise to see someone come to her.

Jean yells at me, "Get me out of this chair and this place. They put me here. I didn't do anything to deserve this."

I respond, "I can help you out of here and take you to a better place. Would you like that?"

Jean, continuing to sound very angry, "I want to get out of here but how do I know you are going to take me to some place better. You might take me to some place worse."

"I guess you will need to believe me, to trust me on that."

Jean is quiet for a few moments then says, still irritated, "Yes, OK, take me to a better place."

I am aware that at some point in the past, Jean had sent a "piece" of herself out—to Jason, her son. She had psychically hooked him, attached herself to him. I understood he didn't know what happened to him, in life or in death, but the effect of it held him down in life.

I say, "First you need to pull back that part of yourself that you hooked to Jason." Jean is surprised I know. She thinks a while, mumbling and trying to get free of the chair. "OK, done," she says as she waves her once stuck hands to break her hold on her son.

Jason is now free of that part of his mother.

Barbara's mother Jean and her brother Jason both died of heart or lung related problems a year apart and her brother, Brad, took his own life a few years later. I was totally surprised to learn that Jean had "sent a piece herself out" to attach to Jason. I didn't understand what that meant, for Jean or for Jason. I hadn't experienced the concept of "sending a piece of a person's self to hook another person." But, the concept became clear to me as we worked together. I was not to take her on to Focus 27 until she disconnected from her son.

I take Jean to Focus 27, the way station for healing. Samantha, my Guide is waiting. To my surprise, Jean's husband, Will, is also there to meet her.

He greets her, "Hello Jean. I'm here to help you to the Healing Center." Jean is quiet. She feels out of her element, out of control, and lost. There is no anger left and she does not know how to proceed. Without the anger boiling inside her, she does not know who she is.

Will and Samantha escort her to the Healing Center.

She goes along passively, like a small child without any particular desire or control.

Will looks back at me and says, "Thank you and give my thanks to Barbara."

Barbara later confirmed that her mother had psychological control over Jason from childhood. He struggled against it during his lifetime and as a result, became controlling and manipulative, treating others as he had been treated by his mother.

With Jean in Focus 27 for help and support, I went looking for Jason. I called his name and connected with him.

Jason is in a small cell with bars on all sides. He is agitated, trying to find a way out. He paces back and forth, moving around the cell, trying to find an opening.

"Where am I? Where am I?" he shouts. "I need help – Help – Help!" He drags his right leg, as if there is something hanging on it. Then, he realizes that the weight is gone. He is looking down at his leg when I come up to him.

I say, "Hi Jason. My name is Judy. Your sister sent me to find you. I can help you get out, if you want."

"Of course I want to get out of here," he answers in an irritated manner.

I wave my hand and the cell disappears.

Surprised, Jason asks, "How did you do that? And what happened to my leg?" He is still irritated but is curious.

"Your cell was a representation of what you experienced in life. You are free of that now."

How did I know that? I just did, with complete certainty. While connected with the Other Side, there is a *Knowingness* that occurs. I do not have a speck of doubt or insecurity, unlike in my normal life in regular consciousness. All interactions have complete transparency on the Other Side of the Veil.

Jason responds, "I don't know where I am. [The environment around him is dark.] God, my leg hurt so much and then the pain went away. I can move without pain. How did that happen?"

The pain in Jason's leg was a metaphor for the psychic pain he experienced from the control by his mother. The way he hobbled from the pain in his leg while attached to his mother represented the way he was hobbled in life from creating an independent existence separate from his mother's control. Because he was controlled by his mother, he wanted to control everything and everyone else around him. That behavior gave him some sense of freedom and independence, no matter the effect on others.

I explain, "You were freed. [It's too complicated at this point to explain his mother's behavior.] Would you like me to take you to a place where you can rest?"

"Yes, please. I'm so tired from the pain and being in that cell. I couldn't find a way out and then the cell just disappeared. Did you do that?" His irritation and bravado are gone and he is like a questioning little boy.

"Yes, I did. Would you like to go with me now?"

Jason response to me: "Yes." He holds out his hand.

I take his hand and we go to Focus 27. Samantha is there with Will, Jason's father. Will says, "Hi son, I can take you to a place where the pain and loneliness will be taken away."

Jason starts crying – such kindness – he never expected that and doesn't feel worthy. But there the Compassion is, in the person of his father. Jason becomes child-like in his countenance – innocent and loving.

After Will comforts Jason, Samantha and Will escort him to the Healing Center. Will telepathically sends me a message that the whole family will be reunited but much healing needs to take place first, for each of them.

My experience in helping many people move from a stuck situation to the healing environment of Focus 27 is that those who are aggressive, controlling and angry become like innocent little children. Their bravado and aggression totally dissipates and they start to become their Essential Selves.

Finally, on to Barbara's other brother, Brad, who died of suicide.

Brad is in a dark place – thick black. He is wandering around crying – so alone and scared. This is not what he expected. He feels like he brought this on himself but he is so lonely and lost. He is crying and whimpering,

Brad says, "I'm so sorry I did this. I didn't mean it. I'm so sorry. Someone, please help me. I'm scared in this place."

He has never felt this lonely before. He thought that killing himself would solve his problems, but this attempt has only made it worse. He feels responsible for this mess and doesn't know how to fix it. He is hoping that someone will come along and take pity on him.

As is the usual case with others who are caught in that mental-loop, people who have died of suicide do not know they were successful in killing themselves. I think this is because they are relatively unconscious to the reality around them on the Earth-Side and see their experience through the lens of a mentally looping mind. This was true of Brad. He thought he was being punished for the *attempted* suicide. He was experiencing what he thought he deserved because he *tried* to end his life.

I enter into his darkness. "Hi Brad. I'm Judy and I'm here to help you."

He is initially shocked to see me – to see anyone. Then he gets down on his knees. "I am so sorry. Can you please help me? I'm so sorry for trying to kill myself. Now I'm in this terrible place." He thinks he is in some terrible place on Earth.

"Yes, I can take you to a better place."

Brad beseeches me, "Oh, please, please..."

I take Brad's hand and lead him to Focus 27. Will and Samantha are waiting. Brad is crying and falls into his father's arms. He is sobbing – feeling such great relief, but also unworthiness, to be out of the awful place. He is just starting to shake the feeling that he really deserved to be in that dark place for trying to kill himself. He still is not aware that he is physically dead.

Will and Samantha escort him to the Healing Center.

As with his mother and brother, Brad will need much help in the Healing Center. But he is where he needs to be and all will be healed—within himself and within the family dynamics.

Anyone stuck spends time in the Healing or Rejuvenation Center after being retrieved. Actually, almost all people who die spend time in the Healing Center to have the debris of the lifetime cleared from the energy that is now their spiritual body. Only those who are enlightened Beings on Earth are without need of healing. When they die, they show up on the Other Side as just pure Light—no form whatsoever—just incredible Light. I have seen a few and they are magnificently radiant Beings.

Will has found other distant family members who died, and has brought each of them to the Healing Center. He helps bring about the healing of the whole family, going back generations. That is part of his role on this side of the Veil.

He tells me to ask Barbara to relax into that fact – Healing is happening with each individual and with the whole extended family. He thanks Barbara for her desire to make this happen. That desire has helped make it so.

Until I met Will, I was unaware that some family members offer a service after death. They retrieve those who have gotten stuck after dying. I wasn't sure why he had not yet done this with his wife and sons – maybe it was to allow Barbara a chance to assist her family. I did have the understanding that Will was helping me in my retrieval of these three family members.

In all situations I have experienced, those who become stuck after death are in the same continuous mental/emotional loop they were in before death. If the person died of suicide, he or she is in the same loop of depression and belief that there are no options left in their life.

If the person died from some other cause but was in a mind-loop of control and aggression over others, they may remain in that mindset after death. The *place* a person finds him or herself in after death is related to either some frightening experience in their life, a belief that they deserve it, or a metaphor for the unchangeable situation of the mind-loop.

Barbara confirmed her mother was very paranoid about others controlling her and had controlled all others in response. Jason spent time in jail which had traumatized him. Brad had been feeling like a victim of circumstances and other people, with no understanding that he had choices in his life. After death, I found each of them in a situation mirroring their greatest fear.

Barbara and I talked about her feelings regarding all of the information. When she asked me to find her family members, neither of us had any idea what might happen for her as a result. She now knew that each one was getting the help he or she needed, and the relationships were Healing.

For Barbara, the burden of responsibility mixed with the guilt of creating a great distance between her family and herself, the blame she felt for herself and others, the guilt of not being able to prevent her last brother's suicide, the profound sadness of a childhood lost and an adulthood barren of her family of origin, all of this was lifted off her shoulders. She was light. She felt light and could see the Light. The whole world looked brighter to her. It was profound Healing for Barbara.

As for me, I was honored to have been of service. What a blessing to help in the Healing of a family on the Other Side, and for Barbara on this side. I learned I could find more than one person at a time, a whole family in fact. I learned that death is no barrier to healing. Healing is always possible.

I was also astounded to learn I was able to accurately understand the relationship connections and dysfunctions. Barbara confirmed this with a description of each family member's issues after I gave her the information. The confirmation was not a surprise to me. I *knew* I was getting correct information because I was doing the work I was meant to do. No worries. No second-guessing of myself, or the information I received. That would come later.

Chapter 10
Magnificent Joy

*Stillness now – profound, precious Stillness – Peace –
being held on Wings of Love. There are people surrounding Karin, people on the Other Side who love her, who
love her for the beautiful Soul she is. Stillness – Peace
– riding a smooth, long wave of profound Stillness.
Being held – being lifted, gliding along on the current of
Stillness. The overwhelming exquisiteness of This. The
immeasurable depth of Stillness, Peace and Joy....*

...My experience of Karin as she is dying

Many months after attending the Monroe Institute and
connecting with people who had died, I had my first
classic Anam Aira experience by escorting a woman to the
Other Side of the Veil at her moment of death. But I didn't
know that's what I was doing until the next day.

I received a call from Kathy concerning her 85-year-old
twin sister dying in Southern California. She was at her
home with around-the-clock caregivers who said she was
not responsive. However, she was agitated and constantly in
motion. Kathy asked me if there was anything I could do to
help her sister, Karin.

I wasn't sure how I could help because I had not connected with someone who was not already dead. I said I

would try.

I tried the same process I used to connect with those who had already moved across the Veil. I was unsure if that would work and I didn't have a Plan B. If this didn't work, I hoped some other way would come to mind. Now I know I receive guidance from the Other Side when I am unsure what to do.

I sat down in my chair at home, put on the Hemi-Sync CD and moved into a meditative state. I went to my cedar home on Focus 27 and mentally called Karin's name. It worked! I was immediately connected to her.

Karin did not want anything to do with me. She told me, in an angry voice, to go away. By her own admission, she said she did not trust people and wanted me to leave her alone. She was irate that I was there and yelled at me to leave her space.

I asked her if I could check on her the following day. She said, "No!" I didn't go away immediately, choosing to hang out with her a while. She seemed to get tired and very irritated at seeing me there but finally reluctantly agreed I could check on her the next day.

With that agreement, I left Karin by just opening my eyes to come back to normal consciousness. I called Kathy to let her know what happened and that I would connect with her sister again the following day.

The next afternoon I checked in with Karin at the Soul level and this is the narrative. As always, I wrote the experience in a notebook as it happened.

I go to Focus 27 and call Karin's name.

She responds immediately and with irritation, "What has taken you so long to get here? [And now sounding relieved] Yes, I will trust you."

I say, "Good. How can I help you?"

Karin, sounding worried, "I am so frightened about dying. I don't know how to do it. I have been such an angry bitch my whole life. I'm afraid I'm going to go to hell – even though I want to believe there is no hell."

I explain to her, "There is no hell – it's only a trap your mind can put you in. It feels like hell but is just a loop of thinking that keeps you stuck."

Karin responds with intensity, "How do I get out of this thinking? It has been this way my whole life. My mind is in control – I can't stop it."

"You can stop believing what your mind is telling you. You are not an angry bitch. You are a sacred precious Being."

Karin, sounding a little irritated, "How do you know? You don't know me."

I continue, "I know we are all precious Beings. You are no different from anyone else on Earth. You are a precious Soul who has been living in a body. That body will not live much longer. But as a Soul, you will continue to live. You will go back to the joy and love you were before coming into body – the loving Being that you are."

Karin, very curious, "How do I believe that?"

I explain, "You don't have to believe it – just allow yourself to know the Truth of it."

Karin, nervous, "How do I do that?"

I say, "Listen to my voice – just listen – focus on what I am going to say. Listen without any judgment. For just this time, imagine that your mind is still. Focus only on the words I am going to say to you. Are you ready?"

Karin, unsure, "Yes …."

In that moment, I was as unsure as Karin. I had no idea what to say that would help Karin relax into this process. Yet, when I started to mentally give her a message of hope, this is what came.

"Karin, you are a precious holy Being – full of Love and Understanding and Compassion for that body you have. That body is not you. You are beyond, above, wholly greater than your body. You are Love – you are Holy – you are an integral part of God. You are Now, you have always been and you will always be."

Karin is silent – listening – barely breathing – taking this in – allowing it to sink into her awareness – into her Soul – into her whole Being.

She starts to cry, a cry of release – release of judgment, anger, distrust, isolation, loneliness, fear. Release of all of her negative feelings toward herself and others for a lifetime.

Stillness now – profound, precious Stillness – Peace – Joy – being held on wings of Love. The immeasurable depth of Stillness, Peace and Joy last for some time. I have no idea how long because it feels like forever. The encounter is so profound I am barely breathing – not wanting to disturb the atmosphere. Such Peace. The Stillness There and the Stillness Here are the same – there is no boundary between Here and There – the profound Stillness that surrounds Karin also surrounds me in my little cottage. Stillness beyond expression.

Karin's family, her parents and the Loved Ones she has known in this lifetime and other lives are surrounding her. They are holding her, hugging her, loving her. She is taking it in – allowing love to fill her… Joy, Peacefulness, Golden Light of Love…

After some time, the experience fades. My cottage and I are back. But I am changed. I know I am, but how, I don't know yet. Everything that makes up my cottage is also changed—the boards, the nails, the foundation, even my dog Sophie sleeping at my feet—everything is different, brighter, cleaner, open....

From that moment, I *knew*—truly *knew*—who we Are—who I Am. I knew and still know, I Am—and everyone else Is—Soul – Spirit – Mind Stream—whatever the descriptor—We Are Beyond All Description.

I was in a state of Ecstasy for many hours that day. I don't remember what I did but I do remember feeling blissed out. No place to go, nothing to do but to be Me—a Me greater than I could ever imagined before *this*. What was *this*? I was not sure—until the next day.

Richard Groves played a video for us during the Anam Cara apprenticeship. In the background of the video were scenes of nature—trees, falling leaves, mountains, streams, oceans, etc. In the foreground was the Bible verse, "Be Still and Know that I am God." Beautiful, peaceful music plays. As the video continued the verse shortened to "Be Still and Know I Am" and then, "Be Still and Know," followed by "Be Still," and finally "BE." I was Being! Just Being. Completely Being.

After I came out of the Bliss state, I talked to Kathy, Karin's sister who told me Karin died at 3 pm, about two hours after I was with her. I thought I probably helped her. It seemed like I did. I didn't have any other explanation for what I experienced. Maybe I was able to prepare her for what was to come when she died.

The following day when I saw Kathy, she told me Karen's caregiver said the Hospice RN pronounced Karin dead at 3 pm the previous day. But that was not the time she died. Her caregiver said she died in quiet peace, a complete change from the agitated, restless state she had been in for weeks. The most astounding thing Kathy said was that Karin actually died at 1:20 pm. I had been working with her from about

1 pm to 1:40 pm. Karin died at the exact time I had that connection with her and the profound Stillness and Joy and Peace. At The Exact Time! Really—at the *exact time* I was with her!

I had become an Anam Aira! The service I desired to fulfill for others since Richard Groves first mentioned it over three years earlier. I had escorted Karin over to the Other Side of the Veil at the moment of her death. I just didn't know that first time I was doing my Anam Aira work!

Since my time with Karin, I have moved over to the Other Side many times with those who have asked me to escort them at their moment of death. Each time is somewhat different, depending on the person's life and readiness to cross over. And each experience is very similar in the profound Light, Love and Ecstasy the person encounters once there.

Many of us are used to seeing and judging ourselves as flawed Human Beings with all our unique, diverse and sometimes troubling characteristics. To be with the person as they begin to comprehend their real identity and as they become aware of the glorious reality on the Other Side of the Veil is Magnificent Joy, for them *and* for me—each and every time it occurs.

Chapter 11
A Visit

From the moment I learned about the concept of Anam Aira from Richard Groves, I understood that a person could escort another across the Veil at the time of death. I thought the type of person who might benefit from help would be someone afraid of dying, someone who did not want to let go of life.

I presumed many people might need assistance based on the significant reluctance our culture has to even talking about death. I saw many patients and families in the ICU who wanted absolutely everything done to save their lives, no matter the cost, financially or physically. There might be a big need to assist people to accept the inevitable—the death of the body.

After escorting Karin across the Veil, I wondered if I would have many other requests for that service. The next week something happened that changed my thinking.

Amanda told me about Bob, a friend of her family, dying of cancer in another state. Bob was about 35 years old and wanted desperately to live. He was very anxious, unwilling or unable to accept the inevitable outcome of his metastatic cancer—death. He refused to relax as long as he was awake enough to move. His family felt he was exhausting himself with his constant movement and agitation, in and out of bed, doing for the sake of doing, all day and most of the night. Amanda wanted to know if I could help him in any way, if I could connect with him at a Soul level because she did not think he would be open to any psychological or spiritual help I could offer over the phone or in person.

Amanda told me that Bob had been very close to his mother, who died of cancer 10 years earlier. Bob was at loose ends after her death until a few years ago. He finally got his life together, finished college, met, fell in love with and married a very special woman. Then, about a year after their marriage, he was diagnosed with Stage Four metastatic cancer. He had all the treatment the doctors thought would help, but the prognosis was grim.

I was not sure how I could help, but I agreed to connect with him at his Soul level. I used the process I applied to connect with anyone's Soul, the same that worked with Karin, when she was still alive. I put on the Monroe CD, moved into a meditative state and called Bob's name.

I was with him, both of us hovering above the home where Bob lived. His Soul told me that he, the Soul, was trying to help Bob come to a state of relaxation but his personality would not listen. I suggested something that just popped into my mind. I wasn't even sure it could be done. I suggested his Soul and I go over to the Other Side of the Veil. Maybe that would get Bob's attention and he would realize what an incredibly wonderful experience awaited him. Nothing to fear. Nothing to resist. His Soul agreed.

Bob's Soul and I move together over the Veil and we come to the Park in Focus 27. Bob's mother is there! She is a beautiful, shimmering Being. She and Bob embrace. They sit on an intricately carved bench and shares what they each have been learning. I stay off to the side so I will not interrupt.

After a joyous time together, several other Beings arrive. Bob is delighted to see many others from this lifetime and other lives. They have a very loving reunion together.

Bob's mother suggests she would like to introduce Bob to the Healing Center. Bob is in the Center for some time with healing Beings – how long, I cannot tell.

One of the processes in the Healing Center is a clearing of the emotional and mental debris that accumulates in the person's energy field during a physical life.

When Bob floats out of the Center, he is sparkling Light. There is Joy and Love and Deep Peace exuding from his very Essence.

Mother shows Bob a blank area within Focus 27 – space undefined and gray – and tells him he can create his own special place Here. It will be waiting for him when he transitions over for the last time. He joyfully creates a most stunning home overlooking a lush valley with a majestic, snow-capped mountain range in the distance.

Bob's Soul is having an incredibly wonderful time. He looks over to me and asks, "May I just stay Here rather than going back to my body?"

I answer, "Yes, you can. Your body will die soon anyway. But if you stay Here, your body will die sooner than it would have if you had rejoined it. You can decide."

Bob's Soul contemplates the decision briefly and then says, "I would like to go back to my body to have as much time as possible with my dear wife and family. I am ready to go back."

Bob and his mother say their goodbyes with Mother assuring Bob she will be with him now and as he finally transitions back to the Park.

Bob and I move back to his body and he sinks in. His body remains asleep."

I called Amanda. She told me she would keep me informed as to how Bob was doing as the days progressed.

About a week later, I heard from Amanda again. Bob died a couple of days earlier. From the day I connected with his Soul and moved him to the Other Side to visit with his mother he had been very different. He woke up from a nap relaxed and calm. He spent his last days loving and being loved by a large group of family and friends. Bob spent quality time with his new wife, a very different situation than the constant motion before his visit to the Other Side of the Veil. No one, including Bob, knew what made the change in his agitated behavior. But, the result was everyone with him during the last days of his physical life had a peaceful and loving time, especially Bob. His passing was gentle and serene.

Initially, I didn't have any clue from where the idea of taking Bob's Soul over for a visit came. It was something completely foreign to me. I know now I have several helpful Guides on the Other Side. There are also the Guides for the person with whom I am connecting at the time. The Guides give me answers to situations I do not know how to handle.

I also understand how the idea of having a Soul "visiting" the Other Side of the Veil can be helpful. But isn't the Soul already There, as well as everywhere? Yes, it is.

Here is how this "visiting" process helps: the Soul and the body are intertwined—Soul, personality and body—deeply linked. Many times in our lives we as personalities go in a different direction than the Soul would want for us. We have free will as personalities and we have lessons to learn as Souls. The personality may seem to be steering us off track from our intended lessons. Yet, there are no coincidences. We may end up learning the negative side of the lesson. An example: if we want to learn about love, but our personality steers us in another direction, we learn about what lack of love is like. If we do something different than the Soul's urgings, we still learn from it.

When I connected with Bob's Soul and took it over to the

Other Side, the Souls of Bob and his mother joined without the effect of Bob's personality. His Soul was then able to bring back the love of his mother and be *heard* or felt by the personality in a deep way. That allowed his personality to settle down and relax into the process of dying, while being aware at Soul level of his mother's assistance.

* * *

After uniting with Bob's Soul, I have often moved to the Other Side with a Soul and come back with them again. Another of these situations was confirmed by someone involved.

Kathy, who owned a foster home for elderly adults, asked if I would connect with one of her residents, Beatrice, to see if there was a reason why she was hanging onto life. She was in a coma and on Hospice Care. The hospice staff thought she would have passed weeks before.

Kathy told Beatrice's oldest son, John, about my Anam Aira work and he supported my working with his mother. From my cottage I connected with the woman's Soul, asking just that question—did she hang on to life for a reason and could we do anything to help?

This is what I received from her Soul:

"One of my sons, Billy, is estranged from the rest of the family. He probably deserves it but I feel so sad for him. He is alone and that makes him all the more angry. I hoped I could bring the whole family back together again before I died. It is my fault I did not get that done. I can't give up my life while he is still outside the family bonds. I want to fix this but I don't know how to do that in my condition."

I suggest I take her Soul over to the Other Side to visit – not knowing how that was going to help. She said yes, she wanted to go.

"OK, hold my hand," I said. Beatrice takes my energetic hand in hers. Off we go. As we land in the Park, she squeals with delight. I look up and understand that the man standing in front of us is the Soul aspect of her estranged son, Billy.

I step off to the side to give them privacy. The two of them talk together for some time. Then they hug and her son walks away. It seems that she has helped him know how to reconnect with his siblings. Beatrice is peaceful now.

I take the Soul of Beatrice back to her body. She enters easily.

I wrote the narrative and drove to Kathy's foster home to give it to her. When I arrived, Beatrice's elder son, John, was there, sitting at the side of her bed as he held his mother's hand. I handed him the write-up of my experience with his mother. He read it. I asked if it made sense to him. He nodded yes, it did. I sat with Beatrice and John for a while and then left. Beatrice died quietly the next day.

About a week later Kathy called to tell me that John came to tell *her* what happened at a family gathering honoring their mother. Billy, the estranged son, came to the gathering, to everyone's surprise. When he walked into the home, he announced loudly to no one in particular that he had a dream the night before their mother died but he didn't want to talk about it. No one pressed him and the only ones who knew about what I had done with their mother were John and his wife.

About a month later, the family held a celebration of their mother's life. John came back to update Kathy. As everyone gathered for the celebration, Billy again joined them. As before, he announced to everyone that he had a dream the night before their mother died but he didn't want to talk about it. John went into another room and brought out the write-up I had given him. He asked his brother to read it. After Billy was finished reading, John asked if that was his dream.

"Yes," Billy said, "I don't want to talk about it."

He handed the narrative back to his elder brother and left.

Kathy never heard from John again so I don't know if things changed for the estranged brother Billy. It's possible that healing may have taken place since the separated younger brother came to both family gatherings. I do hope that happened.

Billy's dream about the visit to the Other Side with his mother surprised me. My Guides and the Guides of the family members were certainly working to bring healing to a fractured family.

How did Billy's Soul find its way to Focus 27 to meet with the Soul of his mother? Our Souls are multi dimensional—*in all dimensions at the same time*. The Souls of Billy and his mother were "present" to experience the healing with each other.

Each and every person with whom I go to the Other Side comes away no longer fearing death. This is a beautiful way to take away resistance and dread. They are therefore not in need of being escorted over at the time of their death. At this writing, I have escorted 14 people over at the moment of their death.

I have taken over seventy people for a visit. They have each died peacefully, hours, days or weeks later. Each of them has connected with Loved Ones on the Other Side. Those Loved Ones stay on this side of the Veil and move across with them at the moment of death. A very natural escort service, indeed.

Chapter 12

Both Anam Cara and Anam Aira

"The Light is Love, Joy, Peace and Freedom and so much more. There really are no words on Earth, in any language, that fully capture the Essence of Light. Light contains everything – is everything. Without Light nothing would exist. With the glorious Light, all – All is possible – All Is."

– A message to Arthur from Joanne, his long deceased wife.

Arthur was an acquaintance, a good friend of my Reiki pal, Sarah. We live in a pretty small town so I had seen Arthur at social events. He was in his 80s and had continued to be healthy and active in his life.

Arthur was very involved in the community. He was a member of two local chorales, a couple of men's groups and was a member of the Tibetan Buddhist sangha.

One day Arthur felt unwell and called 911. By the time the paramedics got to his house, he'd had a stroke. He spent a week in the hospital with early rehabilitation and then went to a nursing home that offered rehab and physical therapy. He was actively engaged in rehab when he had a large heart attack.

Arthur had a pacemaker/defibrillator implanted years before for a chronically slow heart rhythm. That night, the defibrillator went off for the first time, shocking his heart back into a life-sustaining rhythm. The force of the shock knocked him out of bed. He was taken to the hospital. The doctors said he had just survived a large heart attack. He would have died in his sleep if the defibrillator had not shocked his fibrillating and dying heart back to life.

Because Arthur's heart muscle was so damaged from the heart attack, he could not sustain the effort to continue the physical therapy. He chose to go home with around the clock caregivers.

His stroke caused left-sided paralysis and difficulty talking and swallowing. In the few months he lived at home, Arthur could not generate a cough strong enough to clear secretions and fluids from his lungs. He had a couple episodes of pneumonia.

His heart was not able to pump sufficient blood for the energy to do even the simplest tasks without shortness of breath. His failing heart caused him to develop congestive heart failure, for which he had a brief hospitalization.

After those two big health challenges, one right after the other, Arthur was depressed. I offered to help him deal with his grief over all the physical and emotional losses. He said yes, and I began visiting him every few days.

In the tradition of Anam Cara practice, I began with an assessment of Arthur's psychological and spiritual life. He wanted to come to completion without emotional loose ends left unprocessed before he died. Arthur set the pace as we moved through this work. He chose what he wanted to deal with. I helped him with a Life Review and then shifted to forgiveness of himself and others. Because of his Buddhist training he moved rapidly through loss and grief to acceptance.

I started working with Arthur in early January and by early

February, he was ready to consider what dying and the Other Side of dying was like. He heard that I might be able to help him in this area and was open to any assistance I could give him around death and dying.

Joanne, Arthur's wife of 30 years, had died about ten years earlier. He asked me if I could connect with her. I *did* connect with her in the usual way. I typed it up and read it to Arthur on my next visit.

Joanne answers my request to talk to her with, "Yes – Yes – Yes, I am Here, Arthur. I want to give you my hand when you are ready. Judy and I can both bring you over to this side.

"My dear Arthur, how you have grown since I left Earth. You should be very proud of that. You have come into a deeper connection with your own Soul. Like most people on Earth, you still have a ways to go, but your Soul is as close to you as I am – closer, really. You are not quite aware of that just yet. But you will become more aware over time, as you are ready.

"I am so happy you are open to this journey. You are so much more open than earlier in your life. Arthur, my, my, how you have changed, since going West. You could not have become so open if you had stayed in Vermont.

As I read this to Arthur I stopped and asked if these two statements were true. "Yes," he said, nodding his head with emphasis. I smiled and returned to the reading.

"I want you to know how much I love you. I am waiting for you. I have so much to show you – to share with you. You will absolutely love it over Here.

"The Love, the Freedom, the Wondrous Peace – the Joy of the Light. It is the Light – the Light that makes it all possible – makes everything possible. Some call that Light God, Buddha, the Source, or Creator.

"You will be so Happy, Free, and exquisitely Joyful Here in the Space that is The Creator's Home, Our Home. There are so many of your Loved Ones Here, waiting for you, when you are ready. No one wants you to come before you are ready. But we are Here to welcome you, love you and support you upon your arrival."

The content of the message Joanne gave Arthur was one I heard many times as I connected with those who had already transitioned to the Other Side of the Veil. From those who have died to this reality and awakened to what is Beyond, the words may be somewhat different but the feeling and context are the same: Love beyond expression, Light beyond description, and total Joy and Freedom.

I felt joyful as I went back to reading Joanne's words.

"Arthur, I know you have been asking about what it is like over Here. It is more than you can imagine. You will realize very quickly the great Love that you are. You came into this life with the capacity to Love deeply and to experience such profound Compassion. Many have been unable to handle your capacity for Love. And, at times, you also have not been able to handle it. There have been times when you and/or your current partner did not know how to handle the depth of your Love. You have had trouble containing it or channeling it as it was intended, at your core.

"Once on this side of the Veil, you will have no problem with that. The one giving and the one receiving Love does not misunderstand Love. There is a freedom to express the purity of Love and Compassion that is not possible on Earth.

"Arthur, you will be amazed to remember the freedom, the pure unconditional Love of All on this side."

As I continued to read this message to Arthur, I looked up at him occasionally to see his eyes wet with tears and, with one side of his face paralyzed from the stroke, a big half smile lighting up the room.

> *"Arthur, know I am constantly with you at this time. When you are open to it, you will recognize my energy, my Love, my Presence.*
>
> *"Dear Arthur, you are deeply, deeply loved − on both sides of the Veil. We will joyfully welcome you − I will Joyfully and Lovingly welcome you. I am Here with you."*

After I read this to Arthur, he cried for a time, moved and grateful for this connection with his wife. A few days after reading the message from Joanne, Arthur said he could feel his wife with him from time to time—particularly at night. A few days later, he said he could feel her with him all the time.

One day, Arthur asked if I could tell him more about my work. I told him about others I have taken over to the Other Side for a visit. Because he was interested, I read to him from my files of others (with name changes to protect privacy) who had visited the Other Side. Each time I visited, he wanted to hear more about the Other Side. I asked if his wife had taken him over for a visit. He said no and wondered if he could do it. I said I could try to take him over. He was interested.

A few months before, I had taken a course entitled, Using Hypnosis for Those at the End of Life from a skilled hypnotherapist in Ashland. The process of verbally guiding a relaxed person into a hypnotic or meditative state is called "Induction." One of the Inductions the teacher created assists the person with connection to their physical, emotional, mental and spiritual aspects. With her permission, I modified that to include a connection to the person's own Soul. I also added verbal guidance to assist the person in moving to Focus 27 for an experience There.

Using that verbal induction format, I was able to guide Arthur over to the Other Side of the Veil and on to the Park in Focus 27. I sat in silence for a while so he could investigate on his own. After I guided him back to his body, he said he was with his wife and so many others he had known and what a wonderful time he'd had. I was able to see Arthur over There, so I already knew. He was so happy and fell asleep almost immediately after I brought him back to his body.

Arthur asked me a few more times to take him over to the Other Side. Each time I guided Arthur, I was aware of his wife's presence with us. The three of us would go over— Arthur, Joanne and me. During one of those trips I showed Arthur how to create a special place to use after his final transition. He created a stunning home, surrounded by lush vegetation and overlooking a pristine green valley.

Arthur had been home for almost two months. I could see that he was getting physically weaker. After asking me to take him over, he would fall asleep. I connected with his Soul Essence and we would go across, always with his wife present. I hung out to the side of the activity as the two of them happily met with others and then I would bring Arthur back, his wife accompanying us.

Early on, Arthur asked me to be with him at the moment of his transition. His caregivers were instructed to call me when it seemed like he was close to death. I stopped in the day that was to be his last on this side. He was quiet and peaceful. He was not talking any more. He seemed aware of people's presence by his subtle body movement toward their direction but did not interact.

His daughter arrived from Vermont that evening. Arthur roused, visited with his daughter and then talked by phone with each of his four sons. This kind of awaking from a near or complete coma at the end of a life is not uncommon. There is an inner strength that can rouse people to wakefulness to say their last good-byes to their Loved Ones. About 11 pm, Arthur told his daughter he wanted to take a nap and went to sleep. He died in his sleep around 1:30 am. I got the call a few minutes after he passed. I was confident he knew his way over to the Other Side and that Joanne was there to escort him.

After the call, I connected with Arthur by putting on my Hemi-Sync CD and getting into a meditative state. He was already over on the Other Side. This is what I saw and heard:

I see Arthur in the special home he created on the Other Side of the Veil. He is There with Joanne, his parents and so many others who love him. He has the biggest smile. He is so very Happy.

Arthur says, "I did it! I did it! I'm Here! It was so easy, just like you said. I love it Here! I love it!"

Arthur is experiencing great Joy – and yes, total Freedom. He looks to be in his 30s or 40s – very Vibrant, very Happy. Oh, the Joy – the amazing Joy that is Here!

The Golden Light has the texture of Love, the Golden Light is shimmering down on everything and everyone. Arthur is overjoyed. He's jumping around – skipping, singing.

There is a joyful choral group of about 20 floating up to his home – joining him in singing the most heavenly sounds – of Love, of Joy, of Gratitude. There are words and no words – the meaning is inherent in the joyful sounds.

As they sing, the whole place lights up with Love – sparkling, sparkling Love. The singing vibrates the trees – the flowers – the walls of his beautiful home. It seems impossible, but everything and everybody is lighting up with the great Golden Light.

I had attended several of Arthur's choral concerts. They were transporting for us in the audience. But this music was so far beyond anything I knew. It was thrilling. I vibrated with overwhelming Joy.

Love is spreading over everything – Love and incredible Joy. Arthur's Vibrant voice elevates the vibration of everything. Such Happiness and Joy pulsate out and out further. It ripples through the whole area – ripples beyond Time and Space.

There are more and more Beings joining in the singing – to add their Love to the vibration – to the celebration. So much Love is sent out by Arthur and all those who add their energy – their Gratitude to the Whole of Love.

Arthur is lifted up by the music – up into the air. He overlooks the whole expanse of his place – the rolling hills, the brilliant blue ocean, the vibrant mountains in the distance. Arthur is high above it all – he has been lifted by the Love, by the Light, by the Joy of all those who are with him – by Joanne.

Arthur spirals around, singing with such Joy. He is remembering this incredible Love – Love he brought with him into this life, into the life just finished. He is showering that Love back on all of those who Love him here on Earth – to his precious children and their families – to his friends who dearly Loved him over the many years of this past life. He is giving Love and Gratitude to all who are here on Earth – who have touched him, Loved him and helped him.

This is just the very tip of a vast dimension of Love and Light. I know that each of us will experience this. It is our birthright as Souls. This is Where we come from and go back to when we die to this existence.

Arthur is so Grateful – to the whole Universe. Such Happiness cannot be contained. Arthur is spreading and sending and receiving this Joy – this Joy is for everyone – everyone! Arthur feels such Gratitude, for the life he just finished and for all of the lessons received, for all of the help and Love and support he received.

Arthur slowly comes back down to where all of his Loved Ones are waiting. He is aglow with deep, deep Joy. He is that Joy – he is that Love. Arthur is Love. He comes back down with such Peace and Love and Gratitude for All.

Arthur says to me, "Thank you. Send my Appreciation and Love to all."

The scene fades. I am left with a profound Love and Gratitude for Arthur and for All That Exists. It is now 2:30 in the morning and my cottage and I are aglow with Light. I wonder if the astronauts in the International Space Station can see my cottage lit with this brilliant Light?

Chapter 13
Doubt in the Room

From a more Human perspective, Doubt has been my companion from the beginning of this work as an Anam Aira. Sometimes Doubt acts as silent witness, just peeking around the corner. That Doubt is comforting. It helps me stay away from any ego attachment to the Anam Cara and Anam Aira work.

Sometimes, Doubt stands in the room with me, mumbling under its breath. I am not sure what the mumbling words are and I don't want to know. I can, with varying degrees of effort, send it back into the corner and demand quiet. That Doubt feels something like hunger pangs, present and uncomfortable but not life threatening.

Other times, Doubt has stood by and mocked me, "Do you think you are really getting this stuff? I don't think so. I think you are making it up."

And then, occasionally, it has stomped around my cottage, yelling things in my ears like: "What the hell do you think you are doing? You are ridiculous and you are wrong—one hundred percent wrong!"

Nursing was very different. Except for my early years in Critical Care, when none of us were sure what we were doing in this new specialty, I was almost totally without Doubt. I learned my profession well. I taught or guided many hundreds of other RNs in our continuously evolving specialty. Because I wanted to be prepared, I studied each new edition of the latest Critical Care textbooks. I read monthly journals in Critical Care nursing. In different positions within my specialty, whether at the bedside, Critical Care educator or director, I kept abreast of the latest research. I brought that new information to the attention of my peers, administrators and physicians if I felt we needed to change a practice, procedure or protocol.

Practicing the work of an Anam Aira is a completely different experience. Initially (as far as I could tell) I was the only person in the world doing this. For the first few years, I thought Anam Aira work was just about escorting others across the Veil at the time of their death, as Richard Groves described it on that first day of my apprenticeship. But I was not sure what to call the work of connecting with those who had already died, or were soon to die.

According to the Monroe Institute, *retrieval* describes moving *trapped* or *stuck* Souls. But the Institute did not teach how to find people who had died but were not stuck. I continued to connect with many more of those people on the Other Side, because most people just wanted to know that their departed Loved Ones were OK. The Monroe Institute also does not teach how to connect with someone afraid of dying—like those I took to visit the Other Side before their deaths. How did I figure all of this out? I was guided by Spirit to offer these supportive activities.

There are a variety of things I do after connecting with a person's Soul, but each experience involves the same initial process—using the Hemi-Sync CD from the Monroe Institute, getting into a meditative state, moving to the expanded awareness level of Focus 27 and calling the person's name.

In the tradition of Celtic Anam Cara, the term "Anam Aira" referred to those escorting someone over the Veil at the time of death. However, for my own ease, I broadened the Anam Aira definition in my work to include any kind of connection with the Soul. When working with someone alert and preparing for a peaceful death (using techniques I learned in the Anam Cara apprenticeship such as journaling and moving to Forgiveness) I call that Anam Cara.

But other than knowing where I was in any given expanded level of awareness, the Monroe Institute could not help me. And other than knowing the techniques to help a conscious person clear up unfinished business before death, the Sacred Art of Living Center could not help me. I was on my own in discovering what lay behind this practice

There were no textbooks, no best-practice protocols, no one to talk to about my experiences. There seemed to be no one who had any encounters like mine. Sometimes, I was fine with that. Other times, I felt very lonely or out on a limb with nowhere to go but to fall—way down.

***

There have been times I've doubted what I was receiving as I connected with people who died, incidences when what I received didn't make sense or was different than my own Belief System. Doubt and I would decide I had just made it all up—I was creating some story. At those times, I could come up with no other explanation.

The following session with Frederick was one of those times. My connection with him brought up the situation of a person who lived his life through the life of another. I thought that giving up one's own goals and aspirations to live through a partner or relative was a woman's issue. I was sure a man would not present with that kind of problem. It was an issue earlier in my life and I had known many other women who had that tendency. Because I am gay, I don't know men at their psychological core. I knew what my father and brothers were like, and they would never have been dismissive of their own desires, deferring to the women in their lives.

Sara gave me the opportunity to let go of that Belief about men. She asked me to connect with her father, Frederick. She told me her father died several years before. Sara had a difficult childhood in relation to both her mother and her father. Her mother was aggressive and her father passive.

Sara worked with a psychic because she felt he was attached to her even after his death. The psychic was able to help Frederick detach from Sara and move on. However, Sara still felt the relationship with her father was unresolved.

As an Anam Aira, I begin by hearing or intuiting the thoughts of the person I visit on the Other Side. Sometimes the thoughts and conversation are meant for me, and other times I receive a message to be directly relayed to a Loved One still alive, as if the transitioned person was "talking" through me to the Loved One on this side and I just scribed the conversation. I am good at "hearing the verbal interaction" and presenting it as a conversation.

In this connection with Frederick, I sensed what he wanted to convey. In the beginning of the session I felt I was listening in on his thoughts in response to my questions. Later in the interaction, I sensed his connection was with Sara and wrote it down as a direct message to her.

Frederick is at peace. He was connected to you (Sara) before the session with the psychic. That was very helpful to him. He wanted and needed to move on with his experience and learning but didn't know how to disconnect. He thanks you for being with someone who could facilitate that for him and you.

Frederick is now connecting with Guides who are assisting him in understanding the lessons available to him in his Past Lives.

One lesson is understanding how he would get attached to another, like to you before and after his death. This has been a lesson in many of his lifetimes, both as a man and as a woman. He had the characteristic of attaching to and living through another – not recognizing his own self and working on his own life and issues – but rather attaching and experiencing life through another. He had a better understanding of that in this last life, but it was still an issue.

It is helpful for the Loved One left on this side to hear what life lesson their transitioned person was working on in their lifetime. That information helps the Loved One accept situations and behaviors that may have been hurtful or confusing. It can create a healing of the relationship when the Loved One understands the challenges their person had come with into life. Painful situations become less personal and more understandable. For the living person, Compassion and Forgiveness can be the outcome of that knowledge.

As I continued my interaction with Frederick, I understood:

He is now connected with his greater Soul Self, with the help of the Guides, learning the great value and strength of his own Soul. He sees that he didn't need to attach to another person for support and a reason to be. His own Soul has much depth of wisdom, information, and guidance for him.

As I listened to Frederick, I heard more of his story. When he died he went through a Life Review with his Guides, gaining much wisdom about his previous life with Sara.

After transitioning to the Other Side, he understood he had forgotten his way after birth. He forgot how to stay connected with his own Inner Self—his Soul. He saw that this is an epidemic in our world as so many people look for answers outside themselves, looking to others to fulfill and shepherd them through their lives.

His Guides helped him remember his Soul Self, where all the answers lay. He was preparing to come into another lifetime as a Guide, to assist others in remembering to connect with Soul Self while here on Earth. Everyone's answers are within themselves—always and only within.

Frederick says to Sara, through me, "Thank you my dear daughter for freeing me [with the help of the psychic] so I could connect to my Self. Thank you and I say to you – look within yourself – your Essential Self is loving, supportive, compassionate, and wise. It is what you are looking for. Find it within and then you will find a life partner equal to you, matched to you. What Love you will have!"

Frederick continues, "You are going to ask, "How do I do that?" Start talking to yourself, asking for support, asking to be shown your Essential Self. It will happen. Have a continual conversation with your Self. It will soon turn from what feels like a one-way conversation to a dialogue between you and your Soul. Go within – look within – focus within. Your Soul Self is waiting to be heard and felt. Your Soul Self is ready for you.

I love you, dear Sara."

When I finished this session with Frederick, I had a dilemma. My lifelong and unexamined Belief System about the difference between men and women said this could not possibly be true—that a man lived his life through his daughter? Men were not like that!

I considered not giving Sara this information because I was sure she would say, "That is silly. My father was not like that and no man would behave like that."

For a couple of days after connecting with Frederick, I paced around my cottage, trying to figure out how to deal with this—obviously wrong—information about Frederick. I had always found the person I intended to connect with on the Other Side, but I considered telling Sara I could not find her father. Or that I was giving up this line of work and moving to Siberia. I was convinced I just couldn't show up with this ridiculous story.

My own Doubt created great angst. I did not want to give people information I felt I had just made up, and I didn't want to live with the inner Doubt and turmoil I experienced at times like this with Frederick. I remembered decades of confidence in my abilities in nursing. I did not want to live with crippling Doubt doing this work.

But I also did not want to ever bring someone an untruth. I took a very deep breath. With zero confidence in the information I had received about her father, I gave Sara the write-up of my session with Frederick. I waited for the barrage of negative comments from her. To my surprise, she was very relieved.

She told me about her experience with her father over the years of her life. Her father had great expectations for her, about what she would become, the great work she would do in the world and spoke of her physical beauty and skill. As Sara grew into her teens, she realized that her father was living through her. His desires for her were not about her success in the world, but rather about a life he could live through her success. His own life had not turned out as he wanted, and his domineering wife controlled him. He was in a situation he did not know how to get out of. Sara's life was his escape.

Sara came to understand the unhealthy connection with her father. She felt hurt and angered by it. She felt the burden of carrying her father's life. She wanted to get away from that burden.

With the information I received from Frederick, Sara felt vindicated in her feelings about her father's unhealthy attachment, in life and in death. She was freed from feeling she was to blame for that attachment.

Sara also realized that she frequently picked men like her father. She said they didn't appear that way initially, but many of Sara's relationships were with men unfulfilled in themselves, men looking for a woman to complete them, a woman who would take the lead, and help them live the life they wanted.

With the information from Frederick, Sara was able to see the pattern in her life, just like her childhood and early adulthood with her father. She let that pattern go. She did that quickly and for good.

Several months later, Sara called to let me know that her current relationship was with a loving, supportive and actualized man. In it, Sara found a complete partner, and they were happily and joyously loving and supporting each other as equals.

As for me, I went home from the meeting with Sara in a state of wonder. I wanted to remember this crippling Doubt; to remember the outcome of this situation—so different from what I expected. The information I received was correct, when I thought it was so wrong. I realized yet again that I didn't know all there was to know about life—my own or others. And through death, I was getting an education.

I had a Belief about how men were compared to women. But for most of my life, as far as I was concerned, any Belief had no inherent Truth to it. It may be true, it may be partially true or it may not be true. A Belief offers no knowledge or wisdom.

There's a trick to dealing with Beliefs Systems—that of recognizing that one is *in* a Belief System. Many years ago, I heard a description of how Belief Systems come to function in our lives. As we slowly grow from being a baby into adulthood, we unconsciously incorporate Beliefs into our lives.

They come from the many authority figures who influence us. Those Beliefs are like a filler substance in between the scaffolding of our lives. We have to identify—make conscious—those Beliefs and then, we can decide whether to keep them or not.

I believe the scaffolding is our cultural norms we grow up with and, without conscious thought, keep for our own. Those norms are quite specific, depending on where one grows up and if the person lives in a particular locality most or all of their lives. A short example—I was born and grew up in rural Maine until I was 14 years old—a culture of rugged individualism and stoicism. Our family moved to the large industrial, multicultural city of Norwalk, Connecticut—a huge intersection of diverse cultures. For my last two-and-a-half years of high school, we lived in a more rural area outside of that city but the town had no high school. We were bused to the next town, Westport, where many wealthy families lived and worked in Big Business or the Arts in New York City. The culture of privilege was understood and subconsciously inherent within the teenagers I sat next to in high school. Each one of those environments had a very different culture. In the end, it was good. It exposed me to different ways of being in the world. And each of these cultures came with their own Belief Systems.

If we decide to get rid of Beliefs because they don't work for us any more, it can cause a disruption within us. It can be disconcerting, as pulling the filler out causes the scaffolding to shift and maybe feel unstable. Our inner stability will need to reform without the Belief. One Belief can be connected to many others, so the disruption in our inner self can be wobbly as we process.

I received a wonderful lesson that day. My painful Doubt turned out to be what I was making up, not the work. The Doubt was generated by a Belief I didn't even realize I had until then. After recognizing that it was just a Belief, I was able to let it go. I had evidence it was not true. I promised myself to remember this situation and not let myself be hijacked again by Doubt.

Chapter 14
More Than I Could Have Imagined

Samuel was a 90 year-old Jewish man in a small town in Oregon. His early life was much different from the peaceful life he now lived. He was a teenager in Germany when the Nazis came into power. His father was killed early in the Nazi takeover. Samuel lived with his mother, Gertrud, and his sister, Leah, in Berlin trying to stay safe and keep a low profile.

The time came when all the Jews were rounded up in Berlin and taken to camps or prison or immediately killed. Samuel, his mother and sister were not at home when the Nazis came through their neighborhood that day. They were not caught. When they came home later in the evening, there was a sign on the door, marking it a Jewish place. They left immediately. Through friends they were able to find a very small room in which to live and hide in a different section of the city.

The family did not leave the room during the day so no one would see anyone living in that small space. All of their belongings, money and papers were still at their apartment. One or more of them would sneak back to their abandoned apartment to get what they needed. Samuel and Leah snuck their money out and buried it in a cemetery, where they all could have access to it.

One night Samuel's mother went out, maybe to get something from the apartment, but she never came back. Samuel thought she had been caught at their old apartment, because it was being watched. Neighbors were obliged to turn in any Jews.

Although very saddened and worried by their mother's disappearance, Samuel and Leah still had to survive—hiding in the middle of Berlin as two young Jewish teens.

Toward the end of the war, Samuel was caught twice, beaten and tortured but managed to escape both times. Leah was never caught and was free to come out of hiding when the Allies came into Berlin at the end of the war.

Because Samuel was captured, he and his sister were separated for a time. They joyfully found each other when the war was over and immigrated to the United States.

Years afterward, Samuel gained access to Nazi papers related to his mother's death. The papers said she committed suicide and was buried outside the walls of a Berlin cemetery. (It was common not to allow the burial of a person who died by suicide in the "sacred" ground of a cemetery.) After years of searching, Samuel found his mother's grave—outside the walls of an old cemetery.

I met Samuel when his wife asked me to give him some Reiki treatments. He was in his mid-eighties. He had written a small book about his life during WWII for his children, grandchildren and great-grandchildren. He never talked to his wife or children as they were growing up about the war years. Now before he died, he wanted his family to know of his early life.

Samuel gave me a copy of his book one day when I visited. After I read it, I asked him about those days in Germany. He offered more insight into his story. He told me he forgave the Nazis for what they did to him, but he could not forgive them for what they did to his mother. He did not want to forgive. He did not want to forget. And he did not want any more discussion about it!

About six months after my initial visit with Samuel, I went to the Monroe Institute and started my work connecting with those on the Other Side. A few weeks after coming home from the Monroe Institute, I read *Testimony of Light,* written by Helen Greaves. The book was originally published in 1969, a fascinating description of the same Afterlife areas Bob Monroe described in his books and I had experienced at his institute.

The book was a transmission of information by Frances Banks after she died, to her friend Helen. It described Frances Banks' experiences in the Afterlife. Frances was a nun in South Africa for most of her life. She left her order and the Church when her Beliefs no longer felt compatible. Back in her native England, Frances became part of an esoteric church called Churches' Fellowship for Psychical and Spiritual Studies. She developed a friendship with Helen, one of the women in the Fellowship. The two frequently meditated together. When Frances died in November, 1965, she connected with Helen through her meditation within a few days of Frances's death. Frances asked Helen to write down what she dictated. Their connection lasted about 18 months and became *Testimony of Light.*

Frances was involved on the Other Side in retrieving people who had died but were stuck. One was a Nazi officer from a German concentration camp. When she retrieved this man, a woman came along—she was attached to him. As Frances discovered from her, she was a prisoner at the camp controlled by the Nazi officer. She developed a deep hatred of him and because of that hatred, she was energetically bound to him after both their deaths. She was retrieved as he was retrieved. As Frances and others on the Other Side worked with this woman, she was able to forgive the officer and was finally freed from that unhealthy bond.

I thought of Samuel and his unwillingness to forgive the Nazis for the death of his mother. I was concerned he might become attached to the Nazis after his death because of his deep-seated un-forgiveness for what he imagined happened to his mother. I broached the subject with him right after I read the book, but he did not want to consider forgiveness and still did not want to talk about it.

About a year later, I heard that Samuel's slow-growing cancer was beginning to spread aggressively. I asked if I could talk to him about any preparation for dying—my Anam Cara work. He said yes. I asked if he was interested in revisiting the issue of his mother's death and his unwillingness to forgive. He said yes, he was interested.

In all of those years that had passed, Samuel told me, he felt that maybe his mother *had* committed suicide, rather than break under torture and tell the Nazis where her children were hiding. He also worried that his mother was in hell for taking her own life. If his mother had killed herself to protect him, he felt responsible for her death.

Since his mother died early in the war, Samuel also wondered if the Nazis had actually killed her and put it down on paper as suicide, as a way of staining Jewish names and protecting the Nazi reputation. As Samuel told me these worries, he sobbed. He had carried those worries for a long time.

Initially, I thought I would take Samuel through the usual forgiveness work, per Linda Howe's book, *Healing Through the Akashic Records*. But as I contemplated how to help him, I thought if I could connect with his mother, Samuel might experience her as she is now, rather than the image he created of her in the hands of the brutal Nazis. Even if his mother *had* taken her own life, it may have been in protection of her children. I did not think she would be stuck or in some kind of "hell" for that selfless act.

I was able to connect with his mother easily. She was not in "Hell." She was in a wonderful place. And she IS a most extraordinary Being.

I find Gertrud in an exquisitely soft-lit space. This place is very expansive. There are no boundaries. The color around her is a Golden and Sparkling Silver – a soft texture to the space – a puffy softness. Gertrud is in the center of this spacious area. She is glowing with the same soft Light. The Light comes from within her and all around her. There is no differentiation between outside her and inside her.

Gertrud and the Space have a vibrant glow, the glow of Joy and Love and deep, abiding Peace. Gertrud is the pure essence of that Love and profound Joy.

I say to her, "Gertrud, your son, Samuel, would like to connect with you."

Gertrud answers to her son, "Yes I am Here, my dear son. I have much to share with you. Son, I want you to know that I am exquisitely well. I have been so since coming Here. My transition was as it needed to be and of no consequence or trauma – just a transition from that physical life to Love beyond Earthly imagination. My last thoughts were of you and your sister. My last feelings on that side were of the gratitude for my children and the Love – the love I gave and was dearly given. There is no greater Joy than that.

"Dear son, release the images and thoughts you have of my passing. Release the concern. Release the fear. Release the guilt. Release the worry. Release your idea of responsibility to me, and protection of me. They are of your imagination, not the reality. Son, remember my Love for you and your sister. Remember only that, for that is what is important – of consequence."

In her message to Samuel, Gertrud did not address how she died. I have noted that with those on the Other Side the how, when, where, by what means and by whom their death occurred is generally not of any relevance after their transition. It is a means of transitioning from the physical to the non-physical—of no more significance than the importance of a doorway walked though to go from one room to another.

Gertrude continued:

"I met so many of our family and dear friends upon arriving Here. Such a loving welcome. It could not be otherwise.

"Our lives on Earth are as we plan and intend. The life all Humans live – the life you have lived is about opening to profound Love and Compassion – for who we think we are and who we think others are. There really is no difference.

"The lessons – the hard, challenging lessons, when learned have a great reward. The thrill – the exquisite Joy and Celebration experienced Here for the completion of difficult lessons are dearly worth it and are beyond any concept of real difficulty in the larger picture of growth.

"You will see this. You have already experienced it just a little. That is our gift to you; my dear son, and so many more gifts are coming your way.

"You have almost completed an honorable, loving life. You have much to be proud of. You chose a difficult and taxing lesson, and you're in your final phases of loving completion.

"Fear not. Worry not. Be not concerned for me or any of our family and friends. We are in Joyful reunion with each other and All There Is. There is no greater Joy and Reward. There is nothing to desire. There is only the Light and Love of our Being – All Being.

"There will be such celebration when you transition

– Joy, Light, Lightness, and oh, the Love – the profound, ever present, all illuminating Love of All.

"Peace and Love and Light, my dear son. Peace – Love – and the All Present Light of All be with you and your dear wife, Sarah. You have done very well. Your joy and peace will be beyond anything you can now imagine. We will help you tap into it now. Peace, my dear son. Peace and Love, now and always."

As I read this communication to Samuel, he cried, releasing over 70 years of worry, fear, guilt, and not knowing—only imagining his mother in that most frightening of situations. After some time, he looked up, took a deep breath and leaned back in the chair. No words were necessary. He smiled.

As I think about Samuel in writing this chapter, I think he wouldn't have been attached because there were no specific member of the Third Reich in his mind. I was new in this work and didn't understand some of the nuances of situations. It was, in the end, still a very helpful process for him before his own transition.

Later, I checked in with Samuel. He had indeed let go of seven decades of worry and guilt that burdened him. He let go of the image of his mother in a terrible situation and sees Gertrud as she is now—as a most wondrous Being of Light and Love. He arrived at Forgiveness, of himself and of the Nazis. He embraced Forgiveness for everything needing Forgiveness in his life. He was quiet and peaceful within himself. He was free. And he exited this world that way.

Chapter 15
The Arrival of Grace

The death of an animal has always deeply affected me. As an RN for almost 50 years, I was relatively used to people dying. I knew how to steel myself against the heartbreak. For most of my life, I had not lost any close family members, but many companion animals. I was profoundly saddened by that. I had no "steeling of the heart" when it came to animals. I was a complete wreck with the death of each one, even animals in movies or books.

For me, animals of all kinds have a purity, a way of pulling at my heartstrings when they are sick or dying. I have felt an unconditional, loving presence with animals I've never felt from people, myself included. With people, there were often expectations and conditions to accepting me as a Being. I learned that well, and had the same response to others as they had for me—nothing unconditional on either side.

My companion animals were different. Absolute acceptance and love flowed from me to them and back again, a continuous river of appreciation and love.

For three years in a row, 1998 through 2000, I had to have one of my beloved companion animals euthanized. Around Christmas each time. It was a very hard, sad process. I did believe in an Afterlife, for Humans as well as animals. I had also read that Bob Monroe met two of his deceased family cats each time he traveled Out-of-Body. But, believing I would see them again didn't help as I faced putting much loved animals down. My heart was broken each time.

Kismet, my dear Samoyed, had been my companion for several years. She was a pup from a friend's litter, a year old when she came to live with me. From the very first meeting, she seemed much more than a dog. Any time I looked into her eyes a very wise Being looked back. During a meditation one afternoon, Kismet was asleep at my feet. Yet, I was aware of Kismet as a person, maybe in another lifetime, a person who was my support and guide. And I felt that kind of energy from her for the many years she was my companion.

When Kismet was ten years old, she developed breast cancer. By the time she was diagnosed, it had begun to spread. Nothing could be done except to keep her comfortable with pain medication and Reiki. I decided when she could no longer walk up and down the stairs to go outside, I would take her to the vet and have her put down. That day came and I couldn't do it. I carried her up and down the stairs for a few days. She had lost a lot of weight, but she was still heavy. And I was very sad, for she was dying inch by inch.

My partner and I talked to our vet in the weeks preceding Kismet's death. We were with my precious dog in the vet's office when the time came to have her euthanized. The vet put a dog bed on the floor in one of the exam rooms. I sat on the floor and held her as the vet gave her the medication. She was peaceful and it was an enormous relief to me that she was not suffering any more. But I cried for weeks or maybe months. I didn't feel any particular comfort with the Belief that she survived death and was just on the Other Side of the Veil—a Veil I didn't know how to cross.

The following year, our cat Mrs. Putney, had to be put down. She had failing kidneys. We had her from the time she was a kitten. My partner gave this little kitten her name at the time of adoption. Mrs. Putney was a very loving, sweet cat and had grown into her name. It seemed a little strange to call her Mrs. Putney when she was a roly-poly kitten, but as she became an adult cat, the name seemed to fit. She was wise and loving.

It was clear on one visit to the vet that our sweet cat was close to the end. Nothing could stop the kidney failure. We brought her back a few days later. This time, the vet had trouble getting an IV site to sedate her enough to die, having to inject the medication directly into her heart using a long needle. I saw that done many times as a nurse. It was one of the ways to deliver life-saving medication to a patient in cardiac arrest. Still a hard process to watch. Was Mrs. Putney suffering until the long needle finally stopped her heart? I didn't know but I thought she was suffering.

The following year, my beloved and beautiful Arabian horse, Ben, developed congestive heart failure. Ben was boarded a mile from where I lived and I saw him almost daily. Ben was with me for 16 years—longer than any relationship I'd ever had with a person, as an adult. He had seen me through many ups and downs. He was 26 years old—old for most horse breeds but Arabians tend to live well into their thirties. I was counting on that.

Ben was my pride and joy. He was a challenge to ride as he expressed his spirited self while I was on his back. It took all my horsemanship to stay on him at times and I loved that excitement. When I was not riding him, he was a very loving, attentive companion. I read my Robert Monroe books to him in his stall as he ate his nightly hay and grain. He would munch away and frequently walk over to where I sat on a stool in the opposite corner of the stall with my book in hand. He sometimes stood so close to me his head was above mine. I would feel grain, mixed with horse saliva, drop onto my head and slide onto my book. I kept that book with Ben-saliva-ed pages for years.

I went on a vacation for a week in the year 2000 and when I returned, he had fluid below his chest and abdomen. It looked like he had a board on his underside—straight and flat. Ben had a loud heart murmur that both the vet and I could hear without a stethoscope and the board-like effect was from fluid called dependent edema. The vet thought he had ruptured a muscle that keeps the valve leaflet closed between chambers when the heart contracted. Because of that muscle rupture, he was in congestive heart failure.

Although the vet put him on a very high dose (for Humans) of a medication to clear the fluid, it didn't work. With a very heavy heart, the day came when I had to put him down. My partner and I did a relaxing Healing Touch treatment on Ben before the vet came. The treatment, called a Chakra Spread, allowed a person—or horse—to die easily as the chakras were opened wide. The person or animal can release and leave easier—or so was the plan.

I was heartbroken. I didn't want Ben to suffer any more, and at the same time, I was very sad for his dying—for helping him die. When the vet gave him the medication to help him lie down, he couldn't—his legs wouldn't bend because of the edema. He teetered back and forth until he fell over with a loud thud as he hit the ground. I jumped out of the way so he wouldn't fall on me. After he was down, I held his head in my lap as the last medication was given, causing his death.

It was the hardest death I have ever known. Maybe it was because Ben was my first horse since desperately wanting one as a young girl. Maybe it was because he was such a present Being—always his full self, a gem of a Being, a bringer of great Joy and excitement. I was bereft after he died. It took several years to even get near a horse again. Each time I thought about doing that, I cried.

After I moved to Ashland, seven years after Ben died, I met my friend Kathy who had several horses and had rescued many others. I rescued a couple of horses with her and helped care for them. Prince and Princess (my names for them—we didn't know their names) were very sick and we gave them good lives until they died—Prince, six months later and Princess about a year after that. I was sad but, unlike with Ben, I expected those deaths.

Two years after Princess died I went to the Monroe Institute. When I asked for guides to help me retrieve stuck people, it was my beautiful horse Ben and my wise dog Kismet who came with me to help convince those who were stuck to move on to a better existence. I loved having these two special Beings with me while I learned this new skill on the Other Side of the Veil.

I continued the work, including finding people on the Other Side, escorting people over the Veil at the time of their death, taking Souls over to visit the Other Side before dying, and many other ways of connecting with the Other Side of this Life. I had several hundred experiences on the Other Side of the Veil over a four-year period.

During those initial years, I thought I would no longer have sadness at the loss of someone dear to me. What was there to be sad about if I knew where they were and could visit anytime? Yes, that person would not be here in the physical world anymore, but no big deal because I could contact them anytime—all the time.

And then my sweet dog, Sophie died. I had not had a dog or cat or rabbit or hamster or fish or any kind of animal living with me in several years. I met Sophie, half miniature poodle and half American Eskimo, at my friend Sally's home. I fell in love with this little 12-pound bundle of energy and tail-wagging Joy. A year later, Sally, gave her to me because her teenage daughter didn't like Sophie. Sally thought Sophie deserved a place where she could be herself and be loved for that.

And she was—herself and loved for it. Sophie was another special Being—so happy to meet Humans of all sizes and shapes. She shared her enthusiasm for Life with every one she met. She had hundreds of friends and admirers in our town.

Sophie gave me such Joy and Happiness daily. She frequently put her head down on her chair or on the bed, rubbed her eyes and face and came up with her hair going every which-way—like a clown. She looked like she was smiling, pleased she could make me laugh out loud.

Almost every evening, Sophie would wake up from a sound sleep, jump down from her chair, come over to me and start barking. I'd say, "Show me what you want." With that, she ran from me to the cupboard and back to me, back and forth barking, tail wagging.

"Peanut butter?" I asked. Yes, more dancing around, this time in circles and back to the cupboard. There was always a jar of peanut butter on the second shelf. A half a teaspoon of peanut butter later, with my getting the first lick, Sophie settled back down for a nap. Had she been dreaming about peanut butter? I thought so.

I had so much fun with her, including car trips to pretty much anywhere. Each time we went for a walk, she happily engaged with people, butterflies, birds and any other kind of Being—except other dogs. Many people we met on our outings walked away from an interaction with Sophie with happiness on their faces.

And then, after a short, unexpected illness of three days, Sophie died. She had been put on antibiotics for an infected anal gland. Two days later, she became lethargic. I took her back to the vet and her hemoglobin was one-fourth its normal level. The vet didn't know why. Something was destroying her red blood cells—a tumor or maybe an immune response to something—maybe the antibiotic.

I brought her home from the vet's office on Monday after-noon. She could not stand or walk. By later that evening, she could not control her head. It weaved back and forth as she drank a little water from the dish I held for her. She was in her chair I had pulled up next to mine.

About 9 pm, I told her it was OK if she had to leave. But it was not OK with me because I was heartbroken. Yet, I didn't want her to suffer. About 11:30, she looked at me with deep intention. I sensed she wanted me to pick her up and hold her in my lap.

I held her in my arms for an hour. She just gazed into my eyes with the most loving look I had ever seen. Occasionally she looked around our one room cottage like she was taking it in for the last time. Once, she stared at a specific place on the ceiling. Was she seeing Beings who were there for her— were Ben, Kismet, Mrs. Putney, Prince and Princess there? I couldn't tell because I was crying.

As Sophie and I gazed into each other's eyes, she held the gaze. I had to periodically put my head back so I didn't drip on her as I had no tissues and I didn't want to get up with her in my lap. When I looked back at her, there she was, looking lovingly and peacefully into my eyes. After about an hour, she seemed to want to get back in her chair. I curled her up against the back of the chair. About two minutes later, she took two deep breaths and was gone.

I wanted to go with her—I wanted to escort her over as I had with many people—to see her and experience her on the Other Side—but I couldn't. I was crying too hard. I just pet-ted and stroked her. My sweet little girl was gone. And I was here, in an empty house.

I cried for some time. I didn't sleep. I'm not sure now what I did—just looked at her, petted her soft fur and cried, I think. I called several friends when the light of morning came. We arranged to bury Sophie in her aunts' back yard: our friends,

Jean and Kay, who took care of her when I traveled. We chose 10:30 am for several of Sophie's friends to meet at Jean and Kay's place and bury sweet Sophie.

At about 9 am, I put my head back in my chair and closed my eyes.

> *I see Sophie – at my place in Focus 27! She is in the front yard, running around, getting down on her front paws with her back end up – the way she used to play – moving back and forth – sideways – like playing "Catch me if you can."*
>
> *The yard is spacious, sloping down from the house – she is playing on beautiful green grass. She has her cute little body and adorable hair but is also less physical – brilliant light shines through her – Lightness and Joy – Fun – so much Fun and Joy is coming from her.*
>
> *She is playing with a person. The person is darting back and forth as Sophie moves back and forth. Both of them are having such fun – playing – so happy – joyful. Light is also coming from the person – bright Light. Both have incredible brilliant Light shining from their core.*
>
> *As I looked closer at the person, I see that it is me! It is me! I am this shining, Joyful, laughing Being, playing with my Sophie – as we have done so many times.*
>
> *It is amazing to see myself. I have never seen me on the Other Side before. I am the Observer of me and I am the Observed.*

I was already over there when Sophie transitioned! I knew that was true for all of us—that we are in many places at the same time—here on Earth and many areas of the Other Side of the Veil. We *are* multidimensional Beings. But I had not seen it before with my own Self.

Sophie and I were together on this side—the Earth-Side, and we were together on the Other Side, even though I could not consciously transition with her when she took her last breath. What incredible Grace was with me that day! To transform profound sadness to precious Joy. Alchemy was at hand.

I am There playing with my beloved little Sophie, both of us very alive and joyful. At the same time I am sitting in my chair crying, with the dead body of Sophie next to me in her chair.

Incredible Joy on One Side and incredible sadness on the other side, at the same time. Both are real and both are true.

At 10:30, I wrapped Sophie's body in a blanket from the Anam Cara apprenticeship. I took her over to Jean and Kay's. Sophie's friends and I helped dig the hole, I laid Sophie in the grave, we read or said loving things over her and I was the first to cover her with the earth.

I cried a little during this process, but I felt calm and peaceful inside. I knew I would see her again and feel her presence.

I missed Sophie so much. I missed her physical form. I missed her being physically *with* me. I cried easily whenever I thought of or talked about her. Was it any easier to deal with Sophie's death when I knew how to contact her? I wasn't sure some days. And I didn't feel like trying to find her on the Other Side. I would try—but I couldn't. I don't know why. Perhaps because I was deep in the middle of grief.

Almost a month after she died, I was able to check on her.

Sophie, my girl, I see and feel her as amazing Light and Love and Joy. All over – excited and shining her Light everywhere and on everyone. She is Divine – she is – all of these things – sparkling Light – Joyful, Exuberant Energy – Indescribable Love – all over – everywhere.

This is incredible – she is in my heart. There is an amazing Love. She runs in the ethers – form and no form – sparkling, shining Energy – Love and Light rains down on all – including me – including all those who loved her in this Life – Jean and Kay – everyone who knew her and felt her Love.

Waves of sadness – waves of Joy and Laughter – back-and-forth – back-and-forth.

I run with Sophie – in Space – not here – There. We are together – interchangeable energy – flowing energy together – we are shining down, around and all over those who are Here. The sadness is mixed with, and changed, to this shimmering Light and Love.

Here/There—There was no difference between Here and There. It is only in our imagination that there is separation. Sophie was Here, in our cottage, with me—she was Here. I was sad—crying—she was with me—licking the tears away—she was Here with her head on my chest, near my heart, as she had done so often in Life on this side. And I was There with her, experiencing pure Joy.

Sophie is a great Love Being – as we all are. She is – not a species called dog – but a Being of Love and Light and Joy and Freedom – as I am – with her. Sharing the energy of All. It is the Energy – the Light of All There Is. Sophie is That. I am That. We all are That. Every Being in the Universe – we are all That – all of the time – no matter how we are manifesting on a physical plane. We are all That – Light – Truly – Always.

My heart is open – wide – large – cannot be contained – Love and Compassion for all Here on Earth and for all everywhere.

Thank you, Sophie Being – Thank You. Thank You. She gives me a deep nod –

My heart is full. Sadness—yes. And a heart full of Love at the same time.

There was a huge difference for me between my loss of the others, Kismet, Mrs. Putney and Ben, and my loss of Sophie. Yes, after Sophie's death, I was still sad. I cried a lot. I missed her deeply. But now I knew beyond a shadow of a doubt that she and I were still together and would always be. That Truth of togetherness existed when I lost my other beloved companions, but I didn't *know* it—I only *believed* it. To *know* the Truth of non-separation, of no death of our essence; to *know* that we all continue to share the love and togetherness of our Loved Ones for eternity—This is Grace beyond measure.

Chapter 16
Grief and Grace

About the time Kathy and I rescued Prince and Princess, she also rescued a mare and foal. Her daughter wanted to raise the little colt and named him Nemo. He was a couple of months old when he came to live with Kathy and her horses. The geldings in the herd bossed little Nemo around but Prince and Princess were very patient—like grandparents to the little fellow. The babe learned horse manners and gentleness from them. When Prince died, Nemo bonded closer with Princess. They were always together, side-by-side, or Princess leading him from place to place in the pasture.

A year or so after Prince died, Kathy went out to feed the horses and found Princess dead in the pasture. Nemo stood at her side. Kathy called me and I went out immediately. We squatted down by Princess, crying and petting her—she was still warm. As we cried, Kathy put her arm around my shoulders. At that moment, Nemo left Princess's side, walked around behind Kathy and put his front hoof gently on Kathy's back—the three of us connected—arms to hoof. Kathy and I laughed at the surprise and specialness of the moment.

A few minutes later, Nemo ran up onto a small hill about fifty yards away from where Princess was lying as we mourned her. He turned around, faced Princess and gave a very loud, long whinny. It seemed to me he was saying goodbye to Princess—honoring her. When he was finished, he gave a nod, walked down the hill and joined the other horses grazing some distance away. It was the first time he joined the other horses.

I had never seen that kind of behavior from a horse before, but I was also more in-tune with the whole dying experience. At the time, I was in the Anam Cara Apprenticeship and learning more about being with death. I was sad about Princess's death but not devastated. She had been chronically sick since we rescued her. I was open to observing and intuiting meaning rather than being shut down by heavy emotions.

We buried Princess on Kathy's property the next day, placing her in a grave next to Prince, under their favorite apple tree. I went back to the pasture afterward, to see how Nemo was doing. I was still tearful over Princess and was leaning against the fence with my arm up on the top board. As I watched Nemo grazing with the other horses, a new horse, Shasta, walked up to me. She had been abandoned. Kathy rescued her about a week before, but I had not met her. Shasta, a beautiful Appaloosa, stopped right in front of me, laid her head on my arm and closed her eyes. She was rescuing *me*. I decided then to rescue her right back. She was mine to care for as she helped me over my grief for Prince and Princess. Hopefully, I helped her over her grief of being abandoned.

For the next several months, Shasta tended to hang out on one side of a fence that separated two pastures. On the other side of the fence was a very large, white draft horse named Winter. The pasture also held her sidekick Chief: white, older, smaller and blind. He followed Winter everywhere. They were both owned and loved by Joy and Tim. One day Joy asked if it would be all right if Shasta joined her horses in their pasture. She thought Chief was getting ready to die because he had lost weight and was slowing way down in his activities. She saw that Shasta and Winter were already companions across the fence and Joy wanted Shasta to be able to be there for Winter when Chief died.

By the time Chief died some months later, Winter and Shasta had become great companions. Alberto, a black thoroughbred, soon joined them and they were a happy trio for several years.

* * *

I became close to both of Joy's horses but felt especially connected to Winter. Even though she was much bigger than my dear Ben, who had died many years before, she exhibited the same gentleness and care around me as Ben had in our years together.

I looked after the three horses when Joy and her husband Tim took vacations. I loved letting them out of their stalls in the mornings and watching as they all ran, kicking and whinnying, all the way to the far end of the pasture. It was also fun to bring them back in at night to clean stalls, fresh water, hay and grain. It was even fun to clean those stalls because I could imagine the horses laying down in fresh, clean bedding.

In cold weather, I put their blankets on at night. Winter was very tall, as she was part draft horse. Her back was a huge reach for me. On occasion, I mistakenly put Winter's blanket on backwards, with the tail section at her neck. She was very patient as I struggled to position the blanket correctly. Like Ben, she would not move a muscle while I was anywhere near her hooves, even when her blanket was sideways across her back.

* * *

A month after Sophie died, Joy called to tell me she was going to have Winter and Alberto put down the following week. They had both gotten old, and each had been chronically sick, losing weight and vitality. Joy did not want them to struggle through another winter. She gave me the date and time when the vet would be out to euthanize them.

I thought about moving Shasta to a new place before Winter and Alberto were put down. I considered the implications of moving Shasta. Would that protect Shasta from watching her companions' deaths? I knew that all three of them would be upset if one of them were taken away. I didn't want to stress the two sick ones or Shasta. I also remembered my experience with Princess and Nemo. Young Nemo was very aware of the death of his mentor and he handled it better than I did. Or at least he seemed to move on quicker than I did. So, I decided to find a new place for Shasta to live, but leave her with her two companions while they were euthanized. I would be there with Shasta as the vet did his work for Winter and Alberto.

In the week between Joy's call and the day Win and Alberto were to be put down, I found it harder and harder to deal with. I absolutely believed that Joy's decision was right. But my mind and emotions kept returning to my horse Ben, and the pain I had felt over that death so many years ago. I had gotten close to Winter, in particular, while Shasta had been her pasture-mate and I loved her. Maybe it was because she was white and such a gentle Being—much like Ben—that my emotions were taking me back to Ben and *that* pain rather than the somewhat easier and predictable deaths of Prince and Princess.

Losing a close animal companion is very hard, at least for those of us emotionally connected with animals. They give us Unconditional Love and Regard in a way people in our lives may not be able to do. Most animals don't have the mixed up cultural constraints and complications that we Humans have. I experienced great Joy and Happiness from the antics of many of my beloved companions as they were just living their lives in Freedom and, I think, Joy. It is hard to see that vital aliveness end.

My companion animals are very in-tune with me and I with them. And yet, it is so hard to choose euthanasia when it is equally hard to watch them suffer. It is difficult to have a conversation about the pros and cons of euthanasia with my beloved animals. They trust me. Do they understand what I am doing is, in my estimation, best for them? I have hoped they do.

They usually give their permission if we are calm enough to notice it. A look in their eyes, a message that shows up in our mind of their acceptance of the situation, or even dying before we can arrange for the vet to put them down. I have been with friends and seen that internal acquiescence of death as their Loved Beings died. But, there are times when being an Anam Aira for others is a lot easier than being one for myself and my Beloved Ones.

* * *

As each day moved toward *the day* when Winter and Alberta were to be euthanized, I struggled with tears and dread. But I thought, "My God—I am an Anam Cara and an Anam Aira—moving back and forth across the Veil with ease—taking people over for a visit or the final time. No dread—no sadness—ease and peacefulness and confidence in what I am doing for others. But look at me now—crying—stomach in knots—afraid I cannot survive witnessing the horses being put down and ashamed I would not be of any help to my horse Shasta or to my friends, Joy and Tim."

I could do nothing to calm myself. Meditation, walking in beautiful Lithia Park, remembering that I could access Sophie and therefore these two loving horses after they passed— nothing seemed to calm me. It didn't occur to me to ask my Guides for help. I was stuck in a profound emotional spiral, spinning down into an abyss of sadness.

Early in the morning of *the day*, I woke up crying. I looked at the pictures of Sophie, Ben and Kismet in my cottage and pictured Prince and Princess in my mind. I asked for their help. I didn't know what that might be. I didn't really think I would get any help but I didn't know what else to do. And then:

Calm. Peace. Tranquility. Stillness. Love. Compassion. They all showed up almost immediately. Grace had brought them for a visit, just when I needed them. I was back in my Core – my Soul. I remembered the Truth of who I was, who We All Are, Loving Souls who live forever – all of us, horses included.

I drove out to the place where the horses were pastured. In the 30-minute drive, I continued to be calm and focused on my role of helper. The vet arrived. Winter and Alberto were in a pasture separated from Shasta. Joy stood by her great heart-connected horse, Winter. Tim was with Alberto. I walked to the pasture to be with Shasta. Shasta stood facing the others. I stood beside her with my hand on her neck.

Alberto was first. He quietly lay down after the vet gave him the tranquilizer. Tim was with him as the vet gave him the last medication. It was a gentle process. Shasta and I stood near the fence line separating the two pastures and we watched as Alberto took his last breath.

Winter next. She gently lay down with a dose of the tranquilizer. Joy was with her as she remained there. The vet had given the second medication and was listening to Winter's heart with a stethoscope when Shasta let out a very long and loud exhaled breath. Then she bowed her head and kept it bowed for some minutes. Her response seemed very similar to what Nemo did by whinnying towards Princess and then nodding before joining the other horses. I stroked Shasta's neck and back.

When the vet said Winter was gone, Tim opened the gate and let Shasta into the area where the two horses lay. Shasta walked toward Winter, her best buddy, stopped a few feet from her and started to graze. That was it. Joy, Tim and I were calm and so was Shasta.

A little later that day, we took Shasta to her new home with other horses. She quickly connected with a pony in the next pasture. I saw her daily, giving her much attention and love.

About a month later, I found a wonderful new and permanent home for Shasta. For several days before the move, I talked to her and the pony about Shasta's one last move. The pony did have other horses with her. It seemed like she was keeping Shasta company, offering connection to a lonely horse.

Shasta's new home was with a gelding, Romeo and a mare, Delight. Shasta had never been leader of a herd and always seemed fine with being the third of three. It took a couple of weeks for them to become a bonded threesome. I was thrilled that Shasta had a spacious new home and with a new group of friends; horses, dogs, chickens and loving people.

* * *

A most important part of the process of dying is the need to grieve. Even as a Stoic New Englander (although a lot less stoic now) and an Anam Aira, I still needed to grieve each death. Separately. And completely. It is complete when it is complete—however long or short that might be. And sometimes, grief is not complete until we ourselves are on the Other Side again with our Loved Ones. There is no shortcut to grieving, even for an Anam Aira.

We are playing the role of Humans in a physical world, and when we lose someone in that world, there is sadness and a missing of their physical form. Yes, I have connected with Sophie since she died and with Winter and Alberto. I have been with Ben and Kismet many times because they are Guides helping me on the Other Side. I have also been with sweet Prince and Princess and even cute Mrs. Putney.

When I tune into them, I experience them as form and no form at the same time. I know them. I know their energy patterns—I know and feel and intuit and sense them. Within me and around me.

After beginning this Anam Aira work, I had thought that I would not be saddened by the physical death of a Loved One. Still, I grieve the loss of these dear companions, even though I know where they are and can and do go over to visit them. And they visit me here. This is true because, as I have discussed in other chapters, we are multi-dimensional Beings, able to be in all time frames and all levels of existence at once. As our Soul Essence, we are not restricted by *Time* or *Space*.

I was wrong when I thought I would not be affected by the physical loss of someone I love. It is significant because we are in the physical plane. *And*, it is also true we can still have the most loving, precious, continuous relationship with them on both sides of the Veil—because we *are* on both sides, and they *are* on both sides, even if we are not consciously aware of that. That is the Joy and Truth of it.

Chapter 17
More Forgiveness Needed

As an Anam Cara and Anam Aira, I am aware of the necessity of periodic Life Reviews and time at the feet of Forgiveness. The process of Forgiveness is not for the person who did the "deed," although it can help that person. It is more for the person holding the anger and resentment—the pain of the deed. Forgiveness does not mean the responsibility is absolved from the person who did the act. Forgiveness is a process for the pain-holder to help disconnect psychologically and spiritually from the offending action. It is about creating freedom and spaciousness for the pain-holder.

A case study: My big brother Tom was in the second grade and I, a year younger, in the first grade. At the end of one cold winter day in Maine, I remember his walking slowly out of the school building with his head hung low, feet shuffling along the ground. No one was by his side or around him. It looked as if he was the last kid to leave the building.

Several of us kids were down by the road waiting for the bus. One of our friends pointed to Tom and everyone turned around. Someone said softly, "Dumb." Others picked it up and joined in with a chorus of "Dumb," quietly at first, then louder and louder. Laughter, giggles, pointing fingers.

Tom looked up, his face red with shame, his eyes wet with tears. He started running, running home. Running away from shame.

But shame caught up with Tom. It landed hard. It landed for life.

I was one of those kids who shouted, "Dumb!" I felt ashamed immediately after that word came out of my mouth. But it was too late. I'd said it. Shame landed on me, too, that day. Not for life, but it was there for a significant part of it. For Tom, I believe the element of shame ran through his whole life. And the other side of shame, Forgiveness, seemed to be in very short supply within him or for himself.

I was the second-born child in the family and idolized my big brother. I wanted to be where he was and do whatever he did. He was an easy-going big brother and loved to teach me what he learned.

The year Tom started second grade, I entered first grade. I felt more like a peer now, going off to school with him. I was proud he was in the next grade. In front of the whole class, my first grade teacher honored me with praise of Tom's first year. I was Tom's little sister and happy to be so.

In the fall of that year, Tom began having grand mal seizures. I was with him when he had the first one. Tom started shaking, trembling and making strange noises, with spit coming out of his mouth. He was not conscious and I couldn't wake him up. I screamed for Mom and Dad, who came in and held Tom until he stopped seizing.

Because we lived in a small rural town in Maine with few health care services, my parents took Tom to a children's hospital in Boston. He was diagnosed with epilepsy and was given medications to control the seizures—Phenobarbital and Dilantin. It slowed him down mentally—a lot. He was ridiculed as dumb by the kids in school. He stayed back a grade in school that year.

I didn't know what Tom thought or felt about having seizures. We were from strong New England stock. One characteristic of that upbringing is that you don't share feelings—or even admit that you have feelings, instead stuffing them way down inside.

The following school year Tom and I were in second grade together. He was embarrassed to be in the same grade. He continued to struggle academically. I didn't say anything about my own academic successes. Dad frequently tried to help him with his homework, math in particular. Many of those sessions ended with dad yelling at Tom for "not applying himself." Tom would slink off to his bedroom, alone. I felt so sorry for him, wishing I could bestow on him the understanding I had for the same math problems, or English, or whatever challenge he was facing. A few times I tried but he would not let me into his room.

The schools put Tom and me in different classrooms if there was more than one class in the same grade. That helped us but was not always possible. Neither of us wanted to be compared to the other—Tom, because I was smarter, and me, because I felt guilty for being smarter.

Tom found other ways to excel. He got into body building, becoming strong physically. He wanted to be a preacher and practiced giving sermons. In high school, he had the opportunity to preach in our church, a fundamentalist evangelical Christian denomination. He was good at fiery, come-to-Jesus-or-else sermons.

When we entered high school, Tom went to a trade high school and graduated with a high school diploma and a skill as an electrician. I went to a regular high school and took science, Latin and math classes in preparation for going to nursing school.

In 1963, we both graduated from high school. Tom joined the Navy as an electrician and I started nursing school. It was the last time we were in each other's lives in any significant way.

The story of my life over the next several years is addressed in Chapter 3 of *Soul Companion*. I was so caught up in my own life, I don't remember knowing much about Tom's.

The next time I saw Tom was seven years after we graduated from high school. He was out of the Navy and enrolled at Fuller Theological Seminary in Southern California. He had been married for a few years, not happily.

I visited Tom in Southern California for the first time. I fell in love with warm weather, blue skies, and beautiful Pacific beaches with swimmers and surfers galore. I flew to the West Coast in the middle of an East Coast blizzard. About six months later, after the disastrous end of my relationship with Kit and getting fired from my first job as an RN, I moved to California. I settled near my brother because I didn't know where else to go.

Tom had been taken off the Phenobarbital and Dilantin. He excelled academically after he was discharged from the Navy.

We didn't visit one another very often after I moved to California. I was immersed in healing from the previous five years of trauma in my own life. I spent the next five years in therapy with the intention of becoming a straight woman. I did not want to live a life as a lesbian any more. My first experience into the gay lifestyle in Connecticut was devastating. The therapy helped me become a stronger, more self-assured person, but I was still gay. By the end of five years, I stopped therapy and began to accept myself as a lesbian.

I was also trying to figure out what I believed spiritually. I knew I didn't want to have the Belief System of our youth. I settled on agnosticism, because I couldn't say God didn't exist—but maybe He was not a personal kind of God. I thought a more likely possibility was that God was some Being Somewhere beyond Earth, but did not know who I was.

Tom, on the other hand, was attending a conservative seminary to become a representative of a God who was very personal—answering prayers and intervening in Believer's lives.

Tom became a licensed minister in the evangelical denomination of our family. He was developing into a stronger fundamentalist and in my opinion, a chauvinist. He had disdain for women in any position of power or leadership, making fun of his female professors and any female ministers. He had harsh judgment for anyone he thought was below him in intellect or education. I wondered if this was his way of covering that sense of shame from second grade.

Tom became harder for me to be around—loud, opinionated, argumentative, judgmental, controlling, and angry, very angry. About five years after I moved to California, he and his wife moved to Alaska so he could become pastor of a church in Juneau. I saw him rarely.

Years later, I called Tom in one of my rare check-ins. After his first few sentences, I could tell he was in a very paranoid state. In a rambling and incoherent way, he told me his wife had recently divorced him. He had locked himself in their house and was pacing from window to window with a loaded gun in his hand. He seemed ready and very willing to shoot his wife if she came to get anything out of the house. He imagined she had the whole church congregation lined up to invade his home and take everything.

I asked Tom if I could call him back in a few minutes, got off the phone and called 911 in Juneau. I called Tom back and told him that there were people coming to help him. I kept him on the phone until the paramedics arrived, telling him he would be safe with them. They convinced him to go with them to the hospital. He was admitted to the psych unit and stayed for over a month.

I talked with him a few times while he was in the hospital. After he was discharged, he was calm and medicated.

However, he re-emerged as his angry self, always feeling slighted, ignored, and/or emotionally injured by others— always others at fault for his life circumstances.

I watched him from afar and I thought about how his life seemed to have been set in stone by the loss of mental acuity in the second grade—the shame – and the ways he compensated. And there was my own quiet shame for having contributed when I called him dumb.

Even though it was a child's mistake, a few years before Tom died, I processed forgiving myself for that deed done when I was five years old. I also asked for Tom's forgiveness. He didn't remember it and said he didn't have any issues with me.

Tom developed kidney failure. He was on kidney dialysis three times a week for almost a decade. He was not compliant with medications, diet, or any other lifestyle changes that would have helped him. His non-compliance also prevented him from being on a kidney transplant list.

Tom continued to express his anger and resentment, freely heaped on others. But not my father. Tom, like the rest of us siblings, honored and was also a little afraid of Dad. During our childhood and into our adulthood, Dad could become angry and loud. Best not to rile him up.

But, I believed Tom did rile Dad up, at a time when Dad could not talk or express himself. I also *believed* it had very sad consequences for our father—that it led to his death.

* * *

In early September, 2012, our dad had a stroke that left him with left-sided weakness and the inability to swallow or talk. In the years before his stroke, Dad had fallen down many times and his wife, Eva, could not get him up. She had to call neighbors or the paramedics for help lifting Dad off the floor.

While Dad was in the hospital, Tom was convinced that Eva was out to take all Dad's money. As his delusions continued, he imagined she was plotting to poison him.

Dad was getting better and was admitted to a rehab unit. He could walk and use both his arms. He still had problems swallowing and could not talk. He had a feeding tube placed in his stomach. Eva told me he was happy, always a smile on his face. He could laugh and did so frequently as family and friends visited.

In the meantime, Tom's agitation escalated over his belief of Eva's intentions toward Dad. My sister and I strategized ways to get him redirected but it didn't work. One day Tom went to our father's rehab room to tell him the "evidence" that Eva was going to kill him.

As he talked, Tom became more and more angry about Eva and was talking loudly when she came into our father's room. Tom lost any semblance of control and accused her of trying to kill Dad. Tom said our father looked from Tom to Eva, back-and-forth. His interpretation was that Dad was becoming aware of the terrible thing Eva was doing and was shocked. Because Tom was yelling, security guards escorted Tom out of the rehab unit.

Dad could not talk. I don't think our father would have believed Tom. Dad knew Tom's inclination for paranoia and he had tried to help our brother see situations differently.

By that evening, Dad started physically deteriorating, becoming less conscious, until he became completely unconscious a few days later. My sister called my younger brother and me and we hurried to get home to see Dad.

I had moved to complete forgiveness of my father in the summer of that year and was able to spend time alone with him the day before he died. I was free of the resentment I carried most of my life—the resentment of Dad saying I made him sick when he found out I was gay, 40 years earlier.

I was however, beyond angry with Tom. I believed Tom upset our father and Dad could not speak to any of it. I felt Dad had died as a direct result of Tom's actions that day, irrationally laying out his delusional ramblings about Eva. Did I know that to be true? No, I didn't—but I believed it. Belief, however, is not the same as Truth. That concept is a very important distinction in my life as a spiritual seeker. But at that time, it did not help me move to Compassion for Tom rather than reacting to his behavior.

In the middle of the night following my time with Dad, we got the call from the rehab facility that our father had died. My sister and I left immediately for the rehab facility so we could support his wife. I called Tom on the way to ask if he wanted us to pick him up, as we were going to pass near where he lived. He said no. He said he knew Dad was in the arms of his Lord and Tom had helped him get there. Tom was at peace with that.

Dad had not been much of a believer in God or the religion we grew up in. I was angry at Tom's "instrument of the Lord" characterization of himself relative to Dad's Belief in God—or not.

Family members offered to host a dinner for all of us later in the day of Dad's death. Dad had been a surrogate father to many of our cousins and we looked forward to having them together that night.

I was going to confront Tom when he came to the dinner that evening. I planned to yell and swear at him and tell him what a delusional fool he was. I was going to tell him that he killed our father.

I paced around all day, going over in my mind what I was going to say to Tom. By evening all of us, including several of our cousins, were gathered—all except Tom. He had called to say he would be late. I was in the kitchen when he drove up. He had five feet to walk from his car to the stairs leading up to the kitchen. There were four steps up to the kitchen door.

I watched him get out of his car. He had great difficulty walking to the stairs with a cane, and even more difficulty getting up the stairs. By the time he entered the kitchen, he was out of breath and wobbly. His color was ashen. He had an oxygen tank slung over his shoulder and oxygen going into his nose.

With each step he took from the car to the door, I felt more and more compassion for this sad person—a hollow aspect of his former self—that person I had last seen twenty years before. I couldn't yell at him. I couldn't swear at him. I couldn't call him the killer of our father. All I felt was deep compassion and love for this very old-looking version of my big brother.

I was quiet all evening, watching Tom receive compassion and care from everyone. I don't know if he even recognized that caring. At least outwardly, he didn't seem to notice.

I had to fly back home to Oregon before Dad's memorial service. Tom officiated at the memorial, since he was still a minister, by education. My sister said he was confused, walked off, got in his car and drove away without concluding the service.

Since he had alienated Dad's wife, Tom was more alone that ever. Less than a year later, he had a stroke. He recovered most of his movement and could talk, but had trouble with word-finding.

Tom's life was comprised of going back and forth to dialysis. My sister kept in contact with him. I felt compassion for him but I called rarely. Why? I had not forgiven Tom for my belief that he caused our father's death. I discovered that I could hold un-Forgiveness and Compassion at the same time for one person.

In August, 2016, Tom died—alone. He talked to his landlady that morning and was to go to dialysis later in the day. The landlady came by later that afternoon and found Tom dead. There was no autopsy, no definitive cause for his death.

I thought Tom might very well be in his delusional mental loop after death like others I had found who were mentally and emotionally stuck during life. I planned to go find him, but I didn't—for five months. I thought about him. I told myself that there is no time on the Other Side of the Veil so he would not know I didn't come immediately to find him.

In January of the following year, I was ready to forgive and let go of what I thought Tom did to our father, and for the person my brother had become. Clarity over how I hung on to my own Beliefs and Judgments about Tom came to me as I spent New Year's Eve alone, reviewing my previous year. Back to the Forgiveness work I went. It was hard at first. I had to let go of my *Belief* about his role in Dad's death. I had to let go of all judgment—of him, of me, of our lives connected and lives apart.

A few days later, I went to Focus 27 and called his name. This was my experience:

> *I see Tom barricaded in a house – his house in Juneau. He has furniture and mattresses in front of all the doors and windows. He is frantically going from one window or door to another. He has a large rifle in his hands and there are many guns leaning against the furniture. He has piles of bullets on the floor in front of each gun.*

Tom, like our father, had been a hunter earlier in his life so he had many guns and bullets in his home.

> *Tom is yelling, "Get out of here! Get out of here! Leave me alone! Leave me alone!"*
>
> *There's no light coming in the windows. The house is dark except for a small light in another room that barely lights the room where Tom paces. He is frantic and yelling – and he is exhausted.*

In the dozens of stuck people I have retrieved, many seem to be in places with some connection to the lives they have just left.

I step into the room where he is and say, "Hi, Tom."

Tom pivots around and aims the gun at me. He yells, "Who are you? How did you get in here? Get out of here or I will kill you. Get out!"

"Tom, I'm Judy, your sister." We face each other. Tom has the gun aimed at my chest, but he seems confused. He is yelling but is less menacing now.

"Tom, I am here to help you. You don't need to protect yourself anymore."

Tom responses, "What are you saying? I could shoot you right now."

He didn't sound very convincing, and seemed drained. He allowed the gun to lower and it fell out of his hands.

"Tom, I can help you. Do you remember how I helped you many years ago?"

Tom replies, "Yes ... Yes." He is hesitant, his voice quiet.

I continue, "I can take you to a place where you can get help, where you will be loved and taken care of. Would you like that?"

Quietly, he responses, "Yes.." He slumps to the floor, sitting hunched over, mumbling.

I walk over and take his hand. We lift off. Tom looks very surprised. As we land in Focus 27, Dad and my Guide Samantha are there to meet us.

Tom, speaking to Samantha, "My God – Jesus! I thought you had abandoned me."

It's common for retrieved Souls to perceive Samantha or me as someone from their previous lives or a spiritual Being like

Jesus. However we are seen by the retrieved Soul, our focus is to be supportive of the person.

I was surprised that Tom thought Jesus abandoned him. His behavior made more sense to me. If my brother felt like he no longer had the support of his God, no wonder Tom was so angry. I have no idea how long Tom had felt that way in his life.

> *Samantha says, "No, we would never abandon you. We are here to help you and love you."*
>
> *As Tom starts to cry, he looks at Dad and asks, "Is that true? Dad, is that true?"*
>
> *Dad gently says, "Yes, Buck [Dad's name for Tom]. We are here to take you where you will be loved and cared for."*
>
> *Tom looks like a lonely little boy – no anger – nothing left inside of him to prop up his bravado. Dad and Samantha take Tom's arms, and lift him up. He seems to float between them as they take him to the Healing Center. Dad looks back at me and says, "Thank you, Judy. We will take it from here."*
>
> *This is the start of the process for Tom to come back to his essence as a Soul.*

What happened next never happened to me before—or since. I had heard William Peters, a well-known researcher of near-death and shared-death experiences, talk about a son who experienced part of a Life Review of his mother who recently died. The son was shown parts of his mother's life that were helpful in understanding and forgiving her. Was that happening to me? I was not sure. Regardless, it was just what I needed.

> *I now see scenes from Tom's life, from his point of view. So many slights – hurts – seeing the disappointment on*

the faces of Mom and Dad. He can't do better – in math – in reading – in comprehension. He feels like a total failure.

But that can't be. He will show them. He will be the best – physically – and in all ways. He will be a strong man – a preacher with sermons better than anyone.

Inside he feels totally alone, but he is not going to show it. He is not even going to feel it. He will not feel.

But he does – but he can't.

The words come, "It's everyone else's fault. It's the church's fault. There are so many people out there who want to get me. I can't let anybody get me. I am the best! I am the greatest! I am the smartest! I am the most handsome! I am better than anyone else! Yes I am, and everyone is going to know it."

As those scenes fade, I receive a message from my Guides.

"We know you feel sorry and guilty for that time you joined the kids to make fun of Tom. Yes, you could have done better but as a child you acted like the other children acted. You did learn – you did.

"You saved Tom's life later on. He was mentally unbalanced then and became paranoid. Unfortunately he has been back into that state for years."

I ask, "What was Tom's lesson? What was my lesson here?"

"Tom's lesson was to learn to stay connected with his Soul. His Soul – that subtle guidance – could have helped him to get back on the right track – to live a life of Forgiveness and Openness to self, to others.

"Given the challenges he agreed to come in with, it was a hard lesson to learn. All lessons chosen in a life are hard. Tom's last life was not intended to be easy.

"Tom did not learn what he wanted to learn. This does not mean that his life was wasted.

For years, I thought Tom's life had been wasted—that he never developed any self-awareness of how he created the chaos in his own life. I was surprised my Guides knew that, although I should not have been. They do know all I think and feel.

Tom learned the other side of the lesson he came into that life to pursue – what it is like to not stay in touch with Soul. He will have more chances. He will have the help of his Guides, including his father – your father. Your father chose the role of pushing Tom into the lesson. He now will help him learn how he could have done it differently.

"Your lesson concerning your brother is one of Compassion, Forgiveness, and Acceptance – for yourself, for Tom and all Beings. You are getting it."

Forgiveness work is much like peeling an onion—there is almost always more Forgiveness to identify and move through as we come to wholeness within. That was true of the Compassion and Forgiveness I needed to develop toward my older brother, Tom, and toward myself, in reaction to him.

One of the best lessons for me and maybe for all of us, if we are willing, is the glorious fact that Forgiveness can happen after death, as well as before. Death does not limit access and it does not prevent the act of Forgiveness, for ourselves and/or for the one who has passed over, if that is the only time we can be open to it. It is great news indeed.

Chapter 18
Giving Up – Unless...

Aand then, Doubt showed up again—this time, Stomping Doubt. It occupied every inch of my 350 square foot cottage. It also occupied my thinking mind, my increasingly fragile heart and my churned-up gut. Stomping Doubt yelled in my ears, *"What the hell do you think you are doing? You are ridiculous and you are one hundred percent wrong! Your client just said that none of what you wrote sounded anything like his wife's family. How could you do that?"*

I needed no aids to hear Stomping Doubt. But I thought, if I put my hearing aides in, the loud inner voice might go away. It worked with ringing in my ears. But, No—not a chance.

I walked outside into the beautiful garden. Stomping Doubt was there, oozing into more of my body and psyche. I got into my car and drove to the lake just outside of town. I usually love to check out the water level and take a walk with my wonderful dog, Puffin. Still, I felt emotionally and even physically bombarded. There was nowhere to go to get away from the voice. Stomping Doubt was here to stay.

This is what triggered the presence of Stomping Doubt. Timothy had known me for years before and after I began my work in connecting with those who've died. He asked me to connect with his wife's deceased parents. He wanted to give Glenda a message from her parents as a 65th birthday surprise. He said he knew they would have practical guidance, practical help as she transitioned into this new phase of her life.

"Yes, of course, I'd be happy to do that."

I have never received very "practical" messages from the dead, rather messages of Love and Encouragement. I didn't tell Timothy that. If I had, things might have turned out differently.

I put on the Hemi-Sync CD. I went to The Library in Focus 27 and called her father's name.

I received a beautiful message from Glenda's dad. His words encouraged her to connect with her loving Soul, now that she was winding down in her career.

Part of his message was, "My dear Glenda, we know you have completed much of your intended lessons in this life. We are all so proud of you. Now is a time for you to remember and feel how much you are loved on This side of Life. Now you can stop much of your doing and sink into being – just being who you are. Take time to just Be. It will bring you renewed Joy and Energy."

His words were very inspiring and beautiful to me. Great Peace and Love surrounded me as I wrote down his words of Love and Encouragement to Glenda.

Next, I repeated the process to connect with Glenda's mother. Her words were also loving and uplifting. In connecting with her, it seemed like I was in touch with Mother Essence. Her words were Unconditional Love and Regard for her child—giving Glenda total support for the person she had become in the world. I felt her words, her love and her encouragement of Glenda as if she were right in the room with me. In a real sense, she was with me—and I with her.

I felt profound Peace and Joy after receiving these beautiful words from Glenda's parents. I was excited about giving these messages to Timothy as a gift for his wife. I arranged to meet him.

After connecting with a Being from the Other Side, I can go back into that experience immediately, if someone asks me a question about the material I received, like a portal of communication is already open from the initial connection. I can re-access it, as needed, to answer questions from the person on this side. That opening can last from hours to a couple of days. After that, I need to go back to my initial process with the CD, going to The Library and saying the person's name again.

We met at Timothy's home. I let Timothy read what I transcribed. I was there to answer any questions or offer clarification.

As Timothy read the material from his in-laws, a deep frown developed on his face, an angry look in his eyes. After he finished reading, he told me, with an obviously controlled voice, "What you got from Glenda's parents didn't sound at all like them. Any messages they would give Glenda would not be like this. This is not what I expected or wanted for her. I know they would give her practical advice about what to do next in her life, not some flowery words that will not help her."

With tight lips, Timothy said, "I don't believe you really connected in with my in-laws. I think you just made this up."

I was shocked at his response. While feeling shaken, I did not want to get defensive. I explained as calmly as I could, "When I connect with someone, it is the Soul Essence of that person I am communicating with, not the personality that lived a life on this Earth. I generally don't get a sense of the physical appearance of the person on the Other Side or what the person is wearing, or doing—generally nothing related to the personality in the physical life.

"What I do receive is a Soul connection. I may learn what the Soul intended to learn in that life. I learn whether or not the Soul completed those lessons. I also hear deep Love and

Gratitude for those who are still left on Earth. The Soul has typically gone through a Healing Center and a Life Review so there is no anger, resentment, or any other negative emotions left for them to process. There is only Love present."

That explanation did not make a difference to him. He was angry and wanted me to leave. I did.

I don't remember driving home but do remember feeling completely devastated. I was kicked in the gut, I felt like doubling over in pain but I had to drive home. As soon as I got inside, I did double over in pain. But it didn't relieve the anguish weighing down my whole being.

It would be years before I knew how to explain to Timothy my experience and understanding of the process of Soul connection. I didn't have a complete understanding of the process at that time.

I discovered and I have discussed in other chapters what happens if someone is stuck or has a strong Belief about what they will experience in the Afterlife. However, if the person who has died is more open about what happens when they transition, they go to Focus 27. They have a reunion with Loved Ones already passed over. They spend time in the Healing Center clearing the debris of the life just lived. They have a gentle Life Review, assisted by Guides and Teachers.

When the Life Review is complete and all lessons of that life are learned, the Soul rejoins the larger Soul Self, also called the Higher Self or the Soul Essence. The aspect of the Soul then reincorporates into the Soul Essence. All lessons learned incorporate into the Soul Essence. The personality of that lifetime lies dormant within the Soul Essence to be accessed when needed.

For example, because both of Glenda's parents died before her, the Soul fragments that inhabited the people known as Mom and Dad will show up at her reunion when Glenda transitions. She will experience them as her parents.

I am speaking of the Soul as if a section splits off to incarnate into a body to live a life. This is a helpful way to understand the Soul. However, another way to understand is that the Soul Essence is holographic. Any aspect of it is a representation of the whole Soul Essence. Each Soul in a lifetime has access to all lessons learned in all lifetimes, past, present or future—from our perspective. Time in increments called past, present and future does not exist on the Other Side. From that perspective all lives are lived simultaneously. That understanding can be hard to wrap our minds around as we live in Human form.

I wish my understanding of the process had been more complete when Timothy and I had this issue, but I was still learning. It might have helped us both.

I spent days in profound Doubt about what I had received from Glenda's parents. It seemed so real, but Timothy was so unhappy. He was hoping for more concrete guidance to help his wife structure her life after this milestone. He had his own idea of what her parents would say and how they would direct her.

After a couple of agonizing weeks, I decided to take my own trip to the Other Side. I knew there was a real existence on the Other Side of the Veil. I could not deny my hundreds of experiences in Focus 27, The Library or the expanded awareness levels beyond the focus levels Bob Monroe described. That was not what I doubted.

The agonizing Doubt was about me. Was what I received real material when I connected with those who died? Was I making all of that up? It seemed so real. I always felt the deep Love, the brilliant Golden Light, Joy, Freedom and unwavering Compassion as I interacted with those who died to this world. I felt it deeply, viscerally, and clearly. So many of my clients confirmed information I'd received about their Loved Ones. How could I be so wrong with Glenda's parents?

Was I wrong? I needed to know. If I was just making this stuff up, I wanted to stop! And I wanted a life without this incredible pain of Doubt. I did not want to live with Doubt—stomping or otherwise.

I put on the CD and went to my special place in Focus 27, the beautiful home on a bay where my Guide Adventure often counsels me. She often manifests as a gentle, multi-colored whale.

I went down by the bay. Adventure swam up. She had the same multicolored markings I saw on her when we first met. I got in the water and slid onto her back. She slowly swam out to sea. I sat with my head down, body curled forward. I felt shame. She stayed on the surface of the water with me.

I am quiet – thinking, and maybe asking Adventure – asking my Higher Self, the Universe, "When will I ever feel secure in what I receive for people? Do I know I'm getting the real thing? I think I know it but it is a subtle Knowing. It is generally not fireworks – unless I am escorting someone across the Veil – yes, then there are fireworks of Love and Light.

"Am I making this up? I need to know! I want to know! If the answer is "Yes" I am making this up, I am ready to hear it. I will stop this charade immediately, if that is what it is. I do not want to perpetrate a hoax! And I don't want to live with this crippling Doubt any more!"

Adventure understood my second-guessing myself. She gave me space—a gentle trip out to sea, a gentle caring for me.

In my vision, we eventually came to an island—a lush island with coconut palm trees. Gentle waves broke on the shore. I slid off Adventure and walked to the shore.

Adventure joined me as a beautiful woman companion. I can't say exactly what she looked like. I had more of a sense of her rather than a clear picture. She had the same energy as her whale self—loving, wise and very gentle.

We walk towards the interior of the island. I am quiet, still feeling a sense of shame. I look down at my feet, shuffling along. I feel no joy or appreciation of this very idyllic island.

We walk on a wide path meandering among the trees. I see a chest – like a treasure chest from a children's pirate story. It is large and fills the whole width of the path. We stop and I look at the chest. It has carvings that look very ancient, but not like anything I have seen.

The experiences I have on the Other Side of the Veil feel as real to me as any I have in my physical life, much more than a dream. For me, it is REAL. Neurosurgeon Dr. Eben Alexander had a Near Death Experience while in a coma from a massive brain infection. In his book *Proof of Heaven,* and in his talks, he describes the Near Death Experience as "more real than real." I know what he means—it is more real than what we call "reality."

My curiosity is waking up. Adventure encourages me to open the treasure chest. I lean forward and unlatch it. I lift the top of the chest. As I do, Souls float gently out and surround me. I see that they are all the Souls I have helped.

They are the treasure! They are the Treasure of this work!

I hear them all say, as with one Voice, "It is for us that you do this! It is for us, not yourself. Stop looking at yourself, your fears, and your insecurities. It is for us that you have been called. It is the connection you help create between us and our Loved Ones on the Earth-side of Life. Do not look at yourself. Look at us. See our Joy when you connect with us and help our Loved Ones who think we left them behind. Look at our "faces" and see our Joy, feel our overwhelming Joy and Gratitude.

WOW! I could not have made this up because I would not have given myself such an easy out.

"Each time you find one of us on this side of Life, focus on us. Focus on us at the time you connect with us and after the connection. Remember our Joy. Focus on the Service you provide. Think about and feel Gratitude for that Service. Feel humble for being called to this Service. Allow it to infuse your Being and Understanding of why you are doing Holy Work.

"When you notice yourself doubting, change your focus back to any of us, any of the Beings you have helped by retrieving someone or connecting to us for a Loved One. Think about the Beings you help.

"And don't worry about any reactions from our Loved Ones on the Earth-side. As imperfect Humans, we know we are in various stages of understanding the larger cosmos and how it functions. If and when you get a disbelieving reaction from our Loved Ones, understand that they have just not come to the broader understanding of this connection. When you receive negative reactions of Doubt and Disbelief, and you will, focus on us and our Gratitude for your work, not on yourself and your doubt or on any other Humans and their Doubt. Focus on us and our Joy and deep Appreciation for what you have signed up to do. This is the work you have been doing for eons. All of these Souls around you now are so grateful."

As I stood before the treasure chest, with Souls all around me, I was so grateful, so honored to have been of Service. I cried with humble Gratitude.

As each Soul says, "Thank you" to me, they fly off, swirl-ing and twirling – there is incredible Joy all around. Joy beyond belief.

After all the Souls have left, Adventure and I walk back to the shore. I have a spring in my step, my head no longer bent down. She walks into the water and becomes her beautiful, colorful whale-self again. I hop on her back.

Now we are energized. She swims fast – dives with me on her back and then breaches. Swimming down deep and fast and then, swimming straight up – up and out of the water and crash, down on the surface with an incred-ible splash. I hang on.

Over and over and over: down deep into the water and then up and out of the water and then – Bam – back into the water with huge waves. We are Joyful beyond words. I am laughing with Joy I have never felt before. Incredible Joy and Release and Relief and deep, deep gratitude.

What an amazingly Joyful experience – soaring and diving on Adventure's back. I love it! I love the Freedom, the Joy, the sense of abandon of all worry and doubt. I feel – we both feel – Freedom. I really needed this.

Adventure brings me back to my place on the shore. I hop off, feeling Free and Joyful and Hopeful.

"Thank you, dear Adventure." She waves a fluke and swims off, her brightly colored self slipping gently under the water.

I am back in my chair in my cottage. I feel as if I have physi-cally breached with Adventure. I have tears in my eyes and on my face—tears of deep Gratitude. I feel Joyful and Free and Honored to have been called to this work. There is no sign of Stomping Doubt in me, in my cottage, or anywhere in the area. Stomping Doubt has been banished from my psyche.

I am not sure where Timothy is with his Doubt. I know he has had Doubt about many things in his life. Earlier in our friendship he told me he was a skeptical person by nature. I think Doubt is part of the Human condition and part of our work is to come to terms with it. When we Doubt, we are in a state of not knowing who we really are. That is part of our lessons—to remember that we are part of ALL THERE IS— part of GOD.

Has this completely rid me of Doubt? No, but Doubt occurs much less often and at much lower intensity. I sense Doubt occasionally peering around a corner at me. Yes, I know Doubt is there but we are back on easy terms. We can co-exist without any pain on my part—as long as I remember the message I received from those compassionate Souls on the island. Since then, I have taken their advice by focusing on their Joy and Gratitude. It works every time. I am so Grateful for that advice.

I also remember my time with Adventure, relishing the freedom and Exhilaration of the two of us breaching over and over again. The Joy and Pure Ecstasy I experienced is one of the highlights of my Life, even though it did not happen on Earth.

Chapter 19
A Shared Preparation
for Crossing

You ARE – in the midst of cancer – in the midst of cough-ing and trouble breathing – in the midst of being afraid of choking. YOU ARE THE GREAT I AM. YOU ARE US. We are not separate from THAT. You are uniquely qualified to come to Peace, Acceptance and Allowing. You will end this physical sojourn as you lived it – with Curiosity and Wonder.

    – Sam's Soul, coaching him about the end of his Life

Sam and Jane, a couple in their middle years, asked me to work with them when Sam was dying of an aggressive throat cancer. They knew of the Monroe Institute and Sam wanted to prepare for his death by visiting Focus 27 before he died. Jane wanted to support Sam in any way he needed. The three of us began a journey that would be Joyful and Rewarding for each of us.

* * *

There were several "firsts" for me working with this cou-ple. I had not been physically *with* someone I escorted over to the Other Side as they died. With the nine others, I received calls from their Loved Ones saying they had just taken their last breath. I would hang up and immediately connect with the person I was to lead over. I remained in my own home in Ashland. The person with whom I was connecting might be in the same town or another state or country. Distance doesn't matter in this work; it is beyond Time and Space.

I also had not been with someone as they made their choice of when and how to die. The Death with Dignity Act in the State of Oregon allows people with a prognosis of six months or less to live to take a physician-ordered medication to end their Life. The person can decide when and where they die, rather than waiting for the disease to bring their life to an end.

I had not been present as a person took the medication to end their life. I was not quite sure how I would feel, but I did believe in the human right and dignity allowed by the law.

The most thrilling "first" of this experience with Sam and Jane was witnessing a "shared crossing experience." As the dying person transitions, the surviving person is out-of-time-and-space *with* the Loved One as he or she leaves their body. It is likened to a Near Death Experience where a person nearly dies and spends time on the Other Side of the Veil, then comes back to physical life. It changes everything about the surviving person's understanding of Death. They come to truly know that there is no Death. But, in this case with Sam, the surviving person (Jane) is *not* nearly dying.

I learned about the idea of "shared crossing" from William Peters three years earlier at The Afterlife Conference in Portland, Oregon. He was giving a talk on a research program he called The Shared Crossing Project. It involved teaching Loved Ones to have a Shared Death Experience with the person dying.

The concept was first described by Dr. Raymond Moody in a book published in 2010 entitled *Glimpses of Eternity*. Dr. Moody is world renowned for books on the Near Death

Experience (NDE). He has lectured worldwide on NDE for many decades.

Before his first book, *Life After Life,* was published in 1972, no one in the medical community knew about the near death phenomenon—except those who experienced it. And the experiencers were generally not talking about their encounters with the Other Side of the Veil for fear of being ridiculed.

I was the head nurse of a coronary care unit when I read *Life After Life,* shortly after it was published. I was both shocked and curious. How many people, I wondered, had a Near Death Experience as we resuscitated them? No one ever talked to me about it, but I was deep in wonder as I continued to be part of the resuscitation team for many dying patients.

The book rapidly made its way into the medical and nursing communities, and had believers and critics alike. I counted myself as a believer, but I didn't truly "know" it to be true until I visited the Other Side of the Veil at the Monroe Institute decades later.

Dr. Moody interviewed thousands of Near Death Experiencers. Occasionally someone would tell him about being transported to the Other Side of the Veil at the same time a dying person left their body. Sometimes the room changed, or the edges and angles of the room and walls would become nonexistent. Frequently, a beautiful light bathed everything and everyone in the room. Sometimes, the Loved One(s) in the room saw those who had already passed over talking to the person about to die.

The experiences Dr. Moody described in *Glimpses of Eternity* are varied, but almost all of them left the surviving ones feeling calmer and more at ease with the death of their person. As Dr. Moody collected more stories of Shared Death Experiences, he discovered it also happened to doctors and nurses at the bedsides of the dying. In those cases, the medical professional at the bedside of a dying patient had similar experiences as the Loved Ones. Therefore, it didn't seem necessary to be someone deeply connected to the dying person.

It was a spontaneous experience, always a surprise to the one having the encounter. It surprised Dr. Moody, his siblings and their spouses, gathered at the bedside of Dr. Moody's mother. All collectively shared her Death Experience. As Moody wrote in his book, "What should have been one of life's least happy moments was suddenly cause for elation. We had gone partway to Heaven with our mother."

William Peters will write his own book so I won't tell his story. I'll just say he had his own NDEs and years later shared several Death Experiences with patients as he sat at their bedsides as a hospice volunteer.

Because of his encounters with the Afterlife, William set up training programs and a research project involved in teaching others to be open and available for Shared Death Experiences with a transitioning Dear One. He renamed these events Shared Crossings, including encounters with the Loved One before he or she dies, during the death experience, and for an extended period of time after the death.

William and I had several long phone conversations after we met in Portland. He created a training program to teach people like me, as an Anan Aira, to help our clients have a Shared Death Experience. William used his research process with us.

In his protocol, he paired someone assigned as dying person and another as a Loved One. Even with all the work in the Afterlife, I had not experienced dying.

In the training program, William led us through the dying process, first as the dying one then as the Loved One at the bedside. He used a guided meditation process where we imagined our bodies slowing down and stopping, and our

Souls leaving our bodies. Then we imagined being on the Other Side with all the Joy that entailed. I was proficient at escorting someone who left their body, either for a visit or for the last time. But I had not experienced exiting my own body as a dying process. It was a deeply experiential learning that made dying even more personal.

Now I had a chance to help a couple participate in a Shared Crossing. In the spring of 2017, when I met Sam and Jane, Sam was in his early 60s and Jane in her 50s.

Sam was almost six feet tall and thin. I could tell he was muscular before developing cancer. He had a thick head of white hair and a trimmed beard and mustache—a dapper fellow, even with the physical effects of illness. Sam's cancer was extensive. He had been admitted to a hospice service when I met him. He had tumors inside his mouth and throat, which bulged out on both sides of his neck. The tumors grew larger on the inside producing more protrusions on his neck.

Jane also had a strong looking body. She was an avid gardener and from her stories I learned that she was used to working hard physically. Her arms and legs looked like she could handle just about any physical task. Neither of them had a bit of adipose tissue on their body.

There was a painting hanging in their office area which Sam had commissioned of Jane in a hula outfit. She was in a hula dance pose. Jane belonged to a local hula club and said how much she enjoyed that kind of dancing when I asked her about the painting.

Both Sam and Jane had listened to a series of Hemi-Sync CDs from the Monroe Institute. In the weeks before I first met them, Sam read about the Monroe CD series called *Going Home* on the Monroe website. Bob Monroe and Elizabeth Kubler-Ross created the series in the early 1990s to help the dying person as well as their Loved Ones.

The series was on seven CDs each, in two sets, one for the dying and one for the Loved One. Bob's voice guided the dying person to Focus 27 to create his or her own Special Place. That Special Place would be there to visit before they died and as a familiar place to transition to after death. The Special Place is a comforting and restful area in which to get ready to die and to help with a Life Review and Recuperation after death.

Rebecca, a hospice volunteer who knew of me and my work, had been giving Sam and Jane weekly massages. When she heard Sam talk about the Monroe Institute, she put us in touch. I loaned the *Going Home* sets to Sam and Jane after conversation about their use. Soon, Sam wanted to talk to me about the Other Side. He wasn't able to go to Focus 27 just listening to the CDs. I started visiting them, at first every couple of weeks and as Sam's condition deteriorated, several times a week.

At first, Jane, Sam and I had lively conversions about the Afterlife and shared favorite spiritual books. I came armed with one or two of my favorite books about the Afterlife, and usually left with one or two of their favorite books to read.

Their home was up in the hills above Ashland with an expansive view of the valley north of town and the green rolling hills to the east. As I sat with them in animated conversation about the Other Side of the Veil, a group of very large wild turkeys frequently wandered by the windows or several deer grazed under their trees. For me, it was a most beautiful and serene experience—being in the beauty of our place on this Earth while reliving and describing to Sam and Jane the incredibly Shimmering, Magnificent and Loving experience of the Other Side of This Life. It seemed a prefect match—Here and There, wrapped together for us to experience, together.

Sam and Jane had been on a spiritual journey for much of their lives. As a result, Sam was not afraid to die and was interested in experiencing the Afterlife before he died.

Jane was remarkably supportive and focused on Sam's journey through cancer to Death. She was not worried or concerned about how Sam's illness and eventual Death would impact her. She knew she would be alright, although she was not sure how that would happen.

As Sam's cancer progressed, he occasionally became grumpy from pain and the struggle to swallow. Jane responded to Sam like a seasoned nurse and a loving partner, moving seamlessly to get or do whatever he wanted or needed, much of the time anticipating exactly what he wanted before he voiced it.

During some of my early visits, Sam expressed his upset with the fact that he had developed cancer. They lived healthy lives: vegan diet, physically active, focused on healthy, peaceful and joyful inner and outer lives. He never thought he would develop cancer or die young. Six weeks before Sam died, I asked if he would like me to connect with his Soul for an answer to his question, "Why do I have cancer—now or ever—and why am I dying now?"

"Yes!" he said, with no hesitancy.

The message I received was from Sam's Soul, talking directly to him:

Let go of your resistance. Let it drop. As you know, it is not helping you. Focus on the Greater – the Deeper – the Profound.

How does this all work? You are experiencing the last of this particular physical Life, with the Lessons and Knowingness already inside you. Open – Open to the Greater Life – Open to every breath and non-breath – Open to the great Adventure of transitioning yet once again – to Greater Life – to Home – to ALL OF US. You are not alone. You are Loved and Supported from both sides of this very thin Veil – from Us on this side and Jane, Judy and Rebecca on your side.

There is no physical reason why you have this cancer. You could not have done more to prevent it. It is not anything you did or did not do in Physical Life. Allow that Knowing in.

This is about Allowing – Allowing whatever shows up in your life. It is the time to put all you have learned into deep Practice.

This physicality is temporary – we know dying feels like a wall to scale right now but as you look back on it, it will look more like a small stone to step over.

You are getting ready to leave your body. There has to be something to Allow that. It is this – cancer. Any resistance to it – any anger about it will not change this, and you know that.

As I read this to Sam, I occasionally looked up at him—he did not look very happy. His unsmiling face said to me he did not want this cancer nor was he interested in willingly allowing it.

Much literature has been published about how and why people get cancer or other diseases, both from the Western medical point of view and from more esoteric and spiritual considerations. Does it have to do with our high fat, high sugar diets, our stressed out lives, lack of exercise, negative thoughts about ourselves and/or our lives or even others? Yes, a case can be made for any or all of the above. But, none of those were the case for Sam.

I continued reading to him.

This is the time to draw on all you have learned – all you have believed, and beyond that, all you have come to know. This is your graduate school and you are well equipped to master it.

Remember – allowing – acceptance – surrender – to WHAT IS – WHAT IS ALWAYS PRESENT. You are US and We are an Aspect of ALL THERE IS. You Are THAT.

In these times, you may remember your birth into this life. There was a very brief physical distress and then – Pop – you were out – breathing the air of the Earth. It will be much the same as you transition back – a brief experience of distress and then – Pop – back Here – back Home.

I thought of dying as a somewhat similar process as being born. However, this explanation gave me a clearer picture of just how similar the Birth and Death process is from the point of view of the Soul.

In the meantime, allow yourself to travel – back-and-forth – to the body and to Home. It will become more and more natural. You don't have to struggle to get to Focus 27. Take a Breath and Allow – easy – not a determined intention to travel – just an easy, light touch of intention and POP – you will be out of your body and traveling – over Here and anywhere you might like to experience. It is all fine.

This is a very special time in your physical Life – the in-between-Here-and-There. It will be a wonderful final experience of the physical and non-physical as you open to it.

Sam did stop resisting. When I visited, I saw the write-up I gave to him on his clipboard. It looked like it had been folded and unfolded, the edges of the pages wrinkled and worn. He came into Allowing. Then, he signed up for Compassionate Choices, accessing the Oregon law allowing a person to choose the time of their Death.

However, before Sam took that step, there was training for the main event. Sam, Jane and I practiced for the ending of Sam's physical Life and for the Shared Crossing they would experience.

Chapter 20
A Shared Crossing

I see Sam and Jane Joyfully embracing and making loops and spirals – wrapped up in each other.

They Are the Light – the Golden Light of Love, Joy, Freedom and deep, deep Contentment. Their embrace seems to go on and on....

And now they are at a waterfall – the green-blue color and shimmering sparkles come off the water as it cascades down the cliff. They stand under the falls, letting the sparking water flow over them. They are laughing, enjoying the freedom of being Out-of-Body and still connected to each other.

Their love takes them higher and higher – up into the stratosphere. Up and out into the expansiveness of the Whole – experiencing the Limitlessness, the Freedom, the Joy and the all-pervasive Love.

This is part of what I saw as Sam left his body. He was in the active process of dying. Jane was lying next to him. Later, when I shared this message with her, she said there was a sparkling falls on the side of the sacred Mt. Shasta in California where she and Sam spent their first date, camping and romping in the waterfalls and stream flowing from it. It was one of their favorite memories.

A few weeks before Sam died, I began taking Sam and Jane to Focus 27, each of them using a Hemi-Sync CD and my doing a guided mediation over the Hemi-Sync sounds. They both expressed a desire to visit Focus 27; Sam, to see where he would go once he physically died, and Jane, so she would know where to find him after he died. Jane usually lay on a mat on the floor and Sam sat on their couch, propped up with pillows. I sat in a chair between them to keep track of their process and so they could each hear me well.

Sam and Jane each had CDs and ear buds to listen to the Hemi-Sync sounds. We set the sound so thcy could hear the CD as well as my voice as I led them over to Focus 27 in a guided hypnosis process.

Initially, both Jane and Sam had vivid experiences in Focus 27. But as Sam became weaker, he said he went to Focus 27 but could not remember anything that happened. Early on, he had created his Special Place there. As he became weaker, I think he was there with guides administering to him.

Jane, on the other hand, continued to have very vivid experiences—Joyful and Exciting times. She came back to regular consciousness feeling happy and peaceful. I wondered if that helped her stay so focused and present for Sam in her day-to-day care of him.

In the days leading up to Sam's Death, I was with them often, facilitating their trips to Focus 27. The Death with Dignity medication was stored in their kitchen cabinet, ready to be used when he decided. Sam chose a Sunday afternoon to "take the Sacrament" as Jane called the medication that would stop his heart beat and his breathing. On Sunday morning, Jane called to say that Sam was not quite ready. He felt he would be by the next day. He and Jane wanted only Rebecca and me to be there with them. Rebecca had been doing massage and Healing Touch on both of them since he began Hospice Care.

Monday afternoon at 1 pm, Rebecca and I gathered with Sam and Jane. I wasn't quite sure what to expect—what kind of mood they would both be in. But I need not have worried. Sam was hurrying a bit to get ready. He continued to be able to walk around their home even though he was weaker by the day. He was short of breath as he hurried for our 1 pm "appointment" but not significantly so. Jane was getting the CDs lined up to use during the process. They were getting things ready for the "event." No drama, no emotional turmoil.

Sam picked out 2 CDs from the *Going Home* series, one to listen to after he took the first series of medications to prevent nausea and create a relaxed state. He wanted us to put on a second CD once he had consumed the Sacrament. On that CD, Bob Monroe repeated over and over that "it is OK to let go and Go Home. Home is waiting, all is good, there are Loved Ones waiting for you. You are not alone. It is OK to let go and go Home."

Jane created a bed on the floor, in front of their almost floor-to-ceiling windows overlooking the valley and hills of Ashland. Sam wanted to look out at their view as he started this process. He would sit with his back against the couch cushions. Jane would sit next to Sam on that bed as he took the Sacrament and until his body was taken away several hours later.

Jane chose to listen to the Hemi-Sync CD we used during their training. She would listen to it after Sam took the Sacrament. She was going to Focus 27 to wait for Sam.

At 1:30 pm Sam sat down, crossed his legs in mediation style and said he was ready. Kneeling next to Sam, Jane got right in front of his face, they looked at each other lovingly, said some quiet things to each other, then kissed. Jane gave Sam the first series of medications and he drank it down. He closed his eyes and was asleep within a few minutes.

He slept for the hour he needed to wait before taking the Sacrament.

Jane, Rebecca, and I watched Sam and talked a little. Jane was calm and relaxed, just next to Sam as they both leaned back against the pillows. Jane held his hand and stroked his arm. I thought Sam might be in and out of his body several times before finally leaving it behind, and that is what happened. I saw him moving out of his body about forty minutes after he took the medication.

> *2:10 pm – Sam is having periods of lifting out of his body – just a little ways – he is looking into Jane's eyes – he is so very Happy for her Love and Support over all these years. Sometimes he hovers just above his body – he knows he has to stay close in order to take the Sacrament in a little while.*
>
> *He feels such an amazing depth of Love and Peace – only Love and Peace.*
>
> *2:22 pm – Sam has such an open heart for Jane. As he is just out of his body, he talks to Jane, "I Love you beyond any way I can express – you have been my Love for so very long – I am thrilled to be seeing you as I cross over – so Happy, Joyful and Open Hearted."*

At 2:30 pm, Sam awoke as if on cue and was ready to get on with drinking the second mixture of medications—the Sacrament. It was a mixture of several drugs including digoxin to stop his heart, a less expensive option than the sleeping pills that cost several thousand dollars. It was too thick to drink so Jane spent a few minutes diluting it with water. Sam drank it down quickly.

Jane was next to Sam, Rebecca was near him, on the couch and I sat in a chair to his side. I wanted to see what I could experience of Sam as he transitioned.

In less than five minutes after taking the Sacrament,

Sam was deeply asleep. We had to adjust his position so his breathing was not obstructed and he didn't rouse at all.

As I tuned into Sam, I was able to "see" and experience him as he moved out of his body. I wrote down what I saw as it happened, just like when I go to the Other Side to find someone. Here is my experience of Sam:

2:45 pm – a few minutes after taking the Sacrament – Sam is Out-of-Body – just above his body. "I am Free!! I am free!! I am so in love with Jane – with my Life – with all of Life!! I am beyond joyful! I am Free! Oh, my Jane – I love you. I will always be with you."

"I am so Joyful! I wish you [Jane] could be as Joyful as I am! I can run and jump and even do cartwheels.

As he says this, I see Sam running and jumping and especially doing very athletic cartwheels. He is in the space above us, between where we are and the vaulted ceiling.

"It's amazing! Oh, my dearest Jane, thank you so much! I am Free! Thank you so much for helping me become Free!

"Thank you Judy and Rebecca, for being Here – for helping me in this process. Thank you Judy for walking on both sides with us.

"I am Free! My body is breathing but I am not in it any longer. I am laying next to Jane. AND I am zipping around the house!

Wow, he is really zipping around! I can see him moving around the house and even outside. There seems to be no boundary between inside and outside of the house or up or down.

"Oh, I AM, I AM. I know I AM. I forgot that I AM. I forgot. Now I know again. Now I know the Truth again – the whole Truth.

"I want to experience all of who I am but I also don't want to leave Jane.

There is a pause in the connection I have with Sam and then I hear:

"Oh, my Friend, my Guide who has been with me forever is Here. He is telling me I can be in both places – all places at the same time. I can be Here with Jane and I can be on the Other Side.

Jane, Is that you? Are you Here with me? It seems like you are. Oh, We are together over Here. We are! We are! Oh, how I Love you.

I see a combined image—Sam and Jane together, again, without boundaries—no edges between the two people.

Sam is speaking again:

"We are in the Light – the beautiful Light. We are together. I didn't realize we could be this way and my Friend tells me we are also together in our beautiful home. I will be with you Here in our home you manifested for us and we will be on this Other Side also – our true Home.

"We are together everywhere. We are ecstatically Happy! Yes!

"The body is just an illusion of separation. Oh, my God, the Joy we have!"

While I watched and heard Sam, I looked over at Jane. She lay next to Sam, her eyes closed, listening to the Hemi-Sync CD. Within a few minutes of Sam leaving his body, Jane had a big smile on her face. I wondered if she was seeing the same sights I saw with Sam running and jumping and doing cartwheels. She looked so Happy and I was curious.

About 45 minutes after Sam took the Sacrament, Jane took off her headphones. She had a big smile on her face.

She went to Focus 27 and waited for Sam. She didn't see him but she felt an incredible Joy and Freedom and Ecstasy of his presence. She had the same Joy and Freedom and Lightness that Sam was having at the same time Sam was having it. She was indeed in a glorious Shared Crossing with her dear partner.

Jane experienced Sam with her physically, right by her side. He was also very conscious, alive and awake to her, even though his physical body was deeply asleep next to her. Jane experienced Sam in both conditions simultaneously. Yes, we are all on many levels of consciousness at the same time.

I have experienced Souls going into and out of their body many times, before finally leaving the body behind for good. Sam never went back in his body after leaving it about 15 minutes after taking the Sacrament.

Another check-in with Sam almost an hour after taking the Sacrament showed he was now focused more on the Other Side. This time he does not speak, but I am aware of his thoughts and what is happening.

3:20 pm – Now, Sam is with a group of Guides. He is being welcomed – honored – for all he has done – all he has been in this lifetime. He is being honored for his Courage, the Fortitude, Determination, the Wisdom he has earned.

The Group – the Council – is honoring Sam with a ceremony. He is at the head of the table. He is telling the Group what he learned in the Life he just finished. He has learned that Love is the only important feeling – the only important quality. Sam also knows now, "Why the cancer."

He wanted to experience deep receiving before finishing his life. The cancer allowed that – being vulnerable in a way he had not been before, allowing himself to be the recipient of deep caring. That is why the cancer occurred, rather than his dying suddenly of something else.

Sam's heart and breathing continued for about three and a half hours after he drank the Sacrament. He was around his body, Jane and us, as well as on the Other Side of the Veil.

About an hour or so after Sam's heart stopped for good, Jane called the Hospice RN to come pronounce him dead. After spending time with Sam's body, Jane called the funeral home to come for his body.

The following day, before I went to see Jane, I checked in with Sam again. His Soul Essence was fully on the Other Side of the Veil.

Sam, talking, "Yes, I'm Here. This is so amazing – This Side – our Home. Yes, I realize This Side of the Veil is really our Home – all Beings – all Consciousness is at Home Here.

Any other experience in any kind in the physical realm is just an experience. It is not Home – it is not Real Truth – the Ultimate Truth.

All of the other worlds are just for learning and experiencing in ways we cannot do Here. These other worlds give us the opportunity to come back Home with great gifts of learning. But when we are in the moment in physical Life, we think it is real – the real deal – only to be surprised that it is a simulation – just make believe. The lessons are real, that is the Treasure.

Another Treasure is going through the made-up realms with others who are so important to us – like with Jane and me. We were so happy to traverse this life together. What an Honor to have been her partner and I still feel that. I am right at her elbow, not in an interfering

way, only Loving and Supportive. I Honor whatever she
wants to do with the rest of her precious life. I am Here.
I am Loving her. I am available to help her create a little
Magic – or a lot of Magic in her continued physical Life.

Jane continues to feel Sam around her all of the time. She
has not been without him since his physical death occurred.
She has said it feels as if he did not die. She knows he did
not die. He is continuously present with her. A most perfect
Shared Crossing Experience—there seems not to have been
any interruption of Sam's presence in Jane's life—a seam-
less Whole.

Personally, this experience with Sam and Jane has been
a deeply personal journey as well as a universal one. I was
able to use my knowledge and skill as both an Anam Cara
and an Anam Aira more completely than I ever had with any
one client before. That was very gratifying.

Being with and guiding Sam and Jane was Joyful, and
deeply Intimate, so much more Intimate than the many lovely
and cherished moments I have had with dying patients and
their families in an ICU setting.

Each time I met with Sam and Jane, I left Calmer and
more deeply Content than when I arrived. Leaving their home
about 10:00pm the night Sam crossed over, after the funeral
home picked up his body, I stopped and looked up into the
glittering starry sky. My heart felt gigantic—expansive beyond
description. Flowing through me was unfathomable Love and
profound Gratitude for Sam and Jane and Rebecca, for this
work I have been called to and ALL THERE IS. All is truly and
completely right in the Universe.

Chapter 21
At Home – On Both Sides

I am inside an orb – whales! As far as I can see, whales of all kinds and shapes and sizes: a whole Universe inside the orb – the Presence of the whales is overwhelming...

Much I have written in *Soul Companion* concerns travel in the dimensions Robert Monroe called "Human Thought Constructed" areas because that is where most of my Anam Aira work takes me. Over eons, as Humans thought about an Afterlife, realms beyond the physical realms were created by us—Humans—to help our transition to the Other Side of the Veil.

As a reminder of the levels created by Humans, people who have died and are stuck between Here and There can be found in Focus 23. As I have mentioned, they generally don't know they are dead and are trying to interact with some aspect of their Life.

Focuses 24, 25, and 26 are the Belief System territories. People with a strong Belief about what they will experience when they die go to a place matching those Beliefs. They experience what they *thought* they would experience, whether that is a particular form of Western or Eastern religion or something else all together.

Focus 27 is a realm encompassing a broader view of the Afterlife and allows for learning within The Library, another name for the Wisdom of the Ages. It is where those more open to what happens when they die go for recuperation and additional insights. This is where I begin my journeys for others and for myself. According to Bob Monroe, this is the last Focus level created by Humans. Any level or realm beyond Focus 27 is part of the Greater I Am and not defined by Humans. Robert Monroe gave labels to some of those realms but Humans had no hand in their creation. Who created these realms? That is the big question. The answer is, something beyond what we think of as God, Allah, Jehovah or any other name. Perhaps it Is Thought, Source, The Great I Am, All There Is. Maybe it is Light. Love. It is definitely Consciousness, however described. I have not met a Creator in my travels but I know Light and Love and Alive Awareness or Consciousness are representations of IT. And my Soul and every sentient Being's Soul are part of IT.

Beyond the Human Thought Constructed (HTC) areas is where the most incredible and life-altering experiences lay. Most books about Near Death Experiences describe them within the HTC areas. In *The Afterlife of Billy Fingers,* author Annie Kagan receives messages from her brother, Billy, after his Death. Billy's experiences took him far beyond the Near-to-Earth focus levels and out beyond anything our Human minds can make up or describe adequately. Some of Billy's experiences in the Beyond are similar to mine.

My experiences of the Beyond started when I wanted to know where animals go when they die. My beloved Sophie dog, guardian Kismet dog, as well as my beloved horses are at my Special Place on Focus 27. They are There because I wish them There, but they are also in other "places" or existences.

Through frequent visits to the Other Side of the Veil, I know that all Beings have consciousness and are multidimensional in essence. All Consciousness exists in an infinite number of "places" at the same time. Time is always in the Ever-Present Now. Everything on Earth and everything in the whole Universe has consciousness: Humans, plants, trees, alligators, rocks, dragonflies, minerals, bacteria, horses, the Earth herself. And Beyond that, all stars, planets, moons, galaxies and clusters of galaxies have Consciousness.

To experience some of those realms of existence, I began here:

Using my Hemi-Sync CD, I went to The Library in Focus 27 and asked to know where animals go after Death.

I am in an area with huge oval shaped orbs. There are orbs as far as I can see in all directions – in front of me, to all sides of me, above and below me. I receive a Knowing that each of these orbs contains the Soul Essence of animals and other Beings. I feel incredibly small in comparison, a mere inch in height compared to the orbs hundreds of feet tall.

Now I am in an orb closest to me. Whales! Millions or more. I can't tell if the whales and I are in water or air or some other medium – if any. There are whales close to me and whales fanning out farther and farther away – whales the distance of a Universe from me; whales of all kinds, shapes and sizes – species I know and others that look prehistoric and still others that seem from a future time.

I feel – I feel deep, deep Peace – rolling over and within me, and Love beyond description – moving all the way through me as if I am completely permeable. I am completely permeable to all the whales have for me.

Wisdom is Here – the Wisdom of the Ages – eons of existence. I rest in all of This. There is no doing – only Being – we are individual and we are One – we are together as we always have been. Form and no form at the same time. Being-ness exists for – forever – eternity.

After some time I realized I was back in my cottage in a state of profound Ecstasy and a deep *Knowingness* of the Essence of Whale. I felt greatly expanded—as if my Being had the dimensions of the largest of whales. I understood the Heart of Whale.

I had not asked to experience whales but whales have always been important to me. For much of my early life, *Moby Dick* was my favorite book. As I read and re-read it, I discovered that many of my ancestors on my father's side were whalers or builders of whaling ships. Growing up in Maine, I felt a deep kinship with whales. I remember thinking at eight- or nine-years-old that I had come into this Life to make up for the karma (although I didn't know that word yet) of my ancestors who killed whales. It was a strange thought to have as a fundamentalist evangelical Christian, since reincarnation was not a Belief supported in Christian denominations. But it has been with me most of this lifetime.

*   *   *

For a few weeks after my connection with Whale Essence, I pondered what this all meant. Did I exist in a form like the whales—or other forms altogether? Were there orbs for all Beings in physical form?

For those answers, I wanted to connect with my Higher Soul Self. Decades earlier, I read about Robert Monroe's experience of his Soul Essence. It surprised me that I had not tried that.

As I thought about going to the Other Side to connect with my Loving Soul, I was nervous. I had never before been scared or nervous about any journey to the Other Side. I have loved each and every trip to the Other Side of the Veil, and I had never thought I wouldn't want to come back to this side. But would I come back after encountering my Higher Soul?

Before going to the Monroe Institute, I was more interested

in what happened on the Other Side of death than what was happening on Earth. As a nurse, when someone I knew died, I wondered what they knew after dying that they didn't know before. And I wished they could tell me. This desire to know about the Afterlife occurred whether the person who died was a patient, a friend or family member.

If I had been given a choice of living or dying and knowing the secrets of the Universe, I would have chosen the latter. However, to my surprise, since having my first experiences of the Other Side, I have felt a deep appreciation for my Life on this side. I have experienced and continue to know the sweetness of life in a way I never knew before my treks through the Afterlife.

Why? I now know that this time on Earth, in this lifetime, is brief compared to—eternity. I know I have chosen this life, this time, these circumstances, this beautiful planet. All of that gives me Gratitude for where I am and what I am up to, no matter what—yes, no matter what.

As I prepared for the visit to my Soul Essence, I thought about the many books I read about Near Death Experiences. Most of those stories revealed that when the person was "out of their body" and on the Other Side, they didn't want to return to their body and their Life, even when they had a great life and/or small children or other responsibilities.

My dog and companion, Sophie, was still alive at this time. If I had the experience of meeting my Higher Soul Self, would I want to come back for her sake? I might really decide to leave my body behind and it would therefore die. I didn't want someone to find me days later with my poor Sophie alone with my dead body.

I thought my love and concern for Sophie and my commitment as an Anam Aira would keep me grounded enough to come back. Although I was not absolutely sure I would want to come back, I asked my Guides for help in doing just that.

With intention to experience my Great Soul Self, I sat in my chair in my cottage with the familiar Hemi-Sync CD. I took a breath and closed my eyes.

I am in front of a giant orb, as before with the whales – I am looking up at it. There are other orbs in the background but it is this one to which I am totally drawn.

The Orb is brilliant with Light – it is pulsating… Now, I am in It. There is overwhelming Joy Here. The Light is omnipresent – Golden and Present. Love beyond any words to express… This orb is me!!!! It is all Me. It is my Soul – my Essence.

I am Home – like no home we could ever know on Earth – Home – the word – the condition cannot be understood unless one is Here – Home. The Light is within All – The Light is Love and Home and completeness and – Belonging – I am Home where I belong – I have looked for this all my Life. I am overwhelmed with Love and Belonging and Light – no words – I can hardly handle it – Am I going to dissolve? I want to stay aware – Conscious. The Love – I am at Home – the Place – yet I know I Am Home – That is who I am – Home.

The description is really beyond any words or feeling I know how to express. It may seem like I am repeating my experience—the words. How many times can I say, "I am Home?" The encounter with my Soul Self kept reverberating—like being embraced with wave after wave of Home-ness, Belonging. Not just embraced but overwhelmed with Homeness. I don't know how to express that profound feeling and being-state of—Home and Belonging—therefore, repeated words, as I am flooded with wave after wave of Energy—Presence—Beyond words.

Joy is Here – Joy is what is Present – Joy and Love and Light – Freedom – Home – there are no real words to describe This – There is no expression – This is beyond language – This is Being-ness – Home–ness. Presence. Consciousness.

It seems like eternity – Here – I am a one-Being receiving line – hundreds – no – thousands of Beings come past me – touching me. Deeply touching me. I know each of them! – I know them better than I know this person – Judy Hilyard. How do I know them so well?? They are all Me – Soul – Essence – in thousands of lifetimes – they are all me – I greet Sister Mary and all the Sisters – in – in how many lifetimes? The little girl from the burned out church in France is smiling at me. More Beings, male, female, and – other? – more than I could ever count. Beings – Me – in all kinds of dress – and ages – and physical and non-physical existence. All the Beings greet me and I am embraced with Love and Compassion and incredible Knowing and Understanding. I am wrapped and infused – with the most magnificent Being-ness – I Am Home …

Each orb is a Soul Essence. So many orbs for all of Life on Earth—All of Life. All of Life in the Universe.

I experienced my Soul as well as all Souls as orbs of existence. Each Being might describe it differently, based on what we relate to in our physical life.

One Monroe Institute graduate, Bruce Moen, experienced his Soul as a Disk with hundreds of smaller disks coming off the larger one. Each of the smaller disks had a face on it and each face showed emotions. Bruce was an engineer and in his book, *Voyages into the Unknown*, he described his Soul in a way he could relate to.

Back to being with my Soul Self:

The orbs are contained within a larger Force – a larger Life. Love and Life and Joy, beyond imagination. For

All of Life is contained within this Existence. There are vibrations for all kinds of life-forms, physical and non-physical.

This larger Force is an over-arching Life Force containing all of the individual lives – re-imagine the vastness of Complete Life.

This is the Force of Love – Love beyond understanding containing all we know and can conceive of – all we can ever imagine as Life and beyond That.

There is a larger Force beyond That and a larger One beyond That. It goes on into Infinity – Life upon Life – upon Life. Life is Love. Life is Light. The Love/Light is ALL THERE IS –

I float within It ALL. I am a speck – No – I am All There Is. I am within and I AM – ALL. The most Joyful opening – opening – forever – Eternal. I float in the Most Perfect Vibration – no words – no thing.

Then—there is wet—water—on this face—face? What is a face? I touch this face and it is wet with—with tears. This shirt is wet—yes—a shirt—I touch this shirt—my face—the face of Judy—I am in my chair—in my cottage. I have been crying—with what?—Joy—Love—incredible Gratitude.

As I become more aware of being in my cottage, I cry again—I am back in this ordinary reality—I didn't get to choose if I came back or not. I was not asked if I wanted to stay. I felt incredibly sad I was no longer Home.

And yet, as time passes, that experience of Home has never left me. The initial sadness of leaving Home vanished quickly. I have this *Knowingness* – I do know Home now. I Do Belong and I Am Home. Always.

* * *

A couple of years after my experience with the whales and my Higher Self, I had an equally profound journey to the Other Side.

Bob Monroe wrote in *Far Journeys* about an area he called The Aperture where he encountered the souls of people he had known. They had no form. They were pure Light. He connected with them occasionally and had amazing conversations as they waited for what came next. They hung out near an opening they referred to as The Aperture but it was always closed when Bob was there. They told him he could not go through The Aperture because he was still in a body.

These Beings did not know what was on the other side of The Aperture, but they felt they were about to graduate into another realm of existence. Sometimes Bob went back to The Aperture and some or all of the Beings would be gone. They had indeed graduated and he never encountered them again.

I have occasionally met a pure Light Soul. Each was very enlightened—like Sam's mother in Chapter 14. She was full of Love and Light. However, even though I have met these special Beings, I had never seen The Aperture.

During an Afterlife Awareness Conference a few years ago, I attended a session with shaman, Linda Fitch who offered the audience a trip to the Other Side of the Veil while she drummed.

As Linda introduced the process, I wondered what I would like to experience. The idea of seeing The Aperture came to mind. Yes, I wanted to see The Aperture, where Souls hang out before graduating from this Life School to something else. Bob Monroe didn't know what was on the Other Side of The Aperture, and therefore I didn't either. I had no idea about going through it. I just wanted to be where very enlightened Beings hung out.

I sat in a conference-style chair in a large room with two or three hundred other people. Linda was on the stage. As soon as she began to drum, I closed my eyes and mentally expressed the intention to experience The Aperture.

Although I was used to journeying with the sound of Hemi-Sync, the drumming was just as effective.

> *I float up to The Aperture. There is no one else there. The Aperture is open – it is open! It is a huge, round opening, like a single-lens-reflex camera, but a 1000 feet in diameter. I can see – Light coming from inside the opening. The Light is Brilliant – hard to take in, almost painful, so very bright and deeply Golden in color.*
>
> *A thought comes to me, "You cannot go through The Aperture because you are in a body."*
>
> *Then a second thought immediately follows, "That is just a Belief."*
>
> *I am poised just outside the opening. The second thought is followed by a third, "Yes, That is right."*
>
> *Well, OK then. I have a quivering of excitement. A few questions arise: Will I be able to come back through if I enter the opening? Is the Creator on the Other Side? Will I then know the Source of All of this?*
>
> *I am through the opening – not too far in – I can see the opening that would allow me back out and it is still open. I turn away. I am being held, wrapped, supported, Loved. The Light has Presence. It has Texture, It is vibrantly Conscious – the All-Knowing Presence. It is the Knowingness I felt at the end of my pilgrimage on the Camino of Santiago de Compostela.*
>
> *The Light goes on as far as I can see and even further. There is music coming from – Everywhere – so beautiful my heart is breaking open and Love is spilling out and at the same time, washing through me. What is there of me? I don't know. I don't know if I am form or not. I do*

know I Am Light and Love – not separated – Light/Love together. There is no object – I Am. I exist within this Presence, as this Presence – no separation. Only One Existence – One Life... One...

I hear Linda's drum in the distance, bringing me back...

Chapter 22
Significant Answers

As I hone my craft as an Anam Cara and Anam Aira, I see that I have served both functions for myself as well as for hundreds of other people and critters—on both sides of the Veil. My Soul and my Guides facilitate experiential answers on many topics I have long pondered. I describe these as "experiential answers" because they frequently come as my Guides put me in the middle of situations on the Other Side. I experience the answers, rather than the Guides giving me the answers or having them come by thought, reading, or my own intuition. One such answer came very early on.

In 1985, when I first discovered *Far Journeys,* one of the things that intrigued me was what Bob Monroe called The Gathering. His spiritual Guide took him forward in Time and up above the Earth. He didn't know the time of this event, only that it was in Earth's future.

His spiritual Guide took him far out in space, closer to the moon than to the Earth. They faced our planet. As he turned to look at the moon, he was startled to see a huge space ship, motionless, just behind them. It was long and relatively narrow and he estimated it was several miles in length, from stem to stern.

Bob's Guide then took him further out to where the Earth seemed the size of a small star. As he focused, he saw count-less numbers of ships and Beings surrounding the Earth, all focused on that "pale blue dot," as the late astronomer Carl Sagan called our precious planet when it was seen from the Viking 2 probe. Bob received a sense from these Beings that they watched the Earth very expectantly—something of great significance was going to happen and they all wanted front row seats.

Monroe's Guide told him, *"It is what we call The Gathering. These Beings have manifested from nearby energy systems to witness the big show, as you have called it...This big show, which is about to occur, is a very rare event—a confluence of several different and intense energy fields arriving at the same point in your Time-Space. It is this rarity that has attracted so much attention. In terms that you can perceive, it may occur once every 87 million of your Earth years....*

"...The interest lies in the result...One such possibility may alter not only your Time-Space but that of adjoining energy systems as well. Therefore, the wide interest. In Human terms, The Gathering is here to observe the possible birth of a new energy. Will it survive the birth process—or will the energy arrive stillborn?" (from Robert Monroe's *Far Journeys*)

After reading about The Gathering, my biggest question was, "Why did all of those Beings from other energy systems care what happened here? Earth was just a small planet, in a small solar system, in one of billions and billions of galaxies. Even if we blew ourselves up, I couldn't imagine how it could affect other solar systems, our galaxy or other galaxies. And I wasn't really sure what the Guide meant by "energy systems."

What was an energy system relative to a solar system or a galaxy? I now understand energy systems are life existences within our Universe but in different dimensions or frequency, within and outside our known Time and Space.

While at the Monroe Institute in 2013, my final program was called Exploration 27. In the first part of the week-long program, we explored Focus 27 in depth. I particularly loved

The Library and spent much time in it. It was then that I had the incredible experience of The Library opening up onto the Universe. I stepped out into the Universe. I describe that experience in Chapter 6.

The second part of the week in Exploration 27 was two-fold. We were told we were going to The Gathering *and* we would take a journey to the center of the Earth. I was very excited about going to The Gathering because I was fascinated about the idea of life elsewhere in the Universe.

* * *

Trying to control my first-timer's thrilling excitement, and guided by Bob Monroe's voice on the Hemi-Sync CD, I did go to The Gathering that week—the same Gathering Bob had gone to many decades ago. It is still in our future. As I listened to the CD, this is what I experienced during that first trip to The Gathering:

> *This is mind-blowing! I DO see Beings, countless numbers and different shapes and sizes, some without a craft. They are all focused on the Earth. With or without spacecraft, they are floating, totally surrounding the Earth.*
>
> *I know at that moment – WE ARE ABSOLUTELY NOT ALONE IN THE UNIVERSE!!*
>
> *I can see the Earth as if I am in the International Space Station – only much further away. The Earth is Beautiful! The blue-ness, the cloud formations, the land mass are all very vivid and I know—deeply feel—that this beautiful planet is my home, for now. It is much more electrifying than any pictures I have ever seen.*
>
> *The profound feeling as I float among the space ships and other free-floating Beings is one of great Anticipation. Each Being knows how Honored they are to witness an historical event – of Cosmic proportions.*

I floated out there immersed in the sense of Anticipation. I had no other thoughts or feelings—only joined with all the others in the wonder of the moment. Then, I was counted down on the CD—brought back to regular consciousness. It was disorienting to be here—on Earth—at the Monroe Institute—in regular Life. However, I knew we would go back to The Gathering—and—I couldn't wait to rejoin all those others in the great sense of Anticipation.

We went back to The Gathering several times that day. Before the third or fourth trip out, one of our facilitators suggested we try something while out there.

"While you float in space, imagine a full-size mirror in front of you. You see your Human form in the mirror. Now, imagine unzipping your current form and stepping out of it. What do you now see in the mirror?"

"Wow," I thought, "What a great idea!" As I got ready to take the next trip, I eagerly set my intention for the mirror experiment while at The Gathering.

I float among the crowd of spectators awaiting the Big Event. I move a little away from the group. A large oval mirror materializes in front of me. Yes, there I am – looking just like I know myself to be, only less solid. I put my hand up to the top of my head and unzip – not actually seeing a zipper. Nevertheless, my Human form does unzip as I watch.

I step out of the form as it falls away. I am – wow – it is hard to describe. I am a cross between – white, semi-transparent vapor and a delicate white feather – somewhat in the shape of the wing feather of a hawk.

After just being present in my new yet familiar-feeling form, I think, "I wonder where I am from?"

Zoom – I am transported to somewhere – above a planet – an almost totally white planet. At first, I am high up in the atmosphere so I can't see any detail. I float down, closer to the surface of the planet. All of the Beings on the planet look just like – me – they are beautiful, peaceful, serene. I notice the color of the planet is not quite as white – there is color – shades of greens and blues – but muted – pastel.

What do these Beings do here, I wonder?

I am now in a garden-like setting. There are other Beings who look very different from the inhabitants of the planet. I now understand. They are Beings from nearby planets. This planet, and the Beings from here perform a service for the Beings of all the other planets in the system. They are Healers – like I am back home on Earth, with Reiki, Healing Touch and even my Anam Cara and Anam Aira work.

On this planet, the Beings use another form of energetic healing I can't describe, but is healing nonetheless. They are the Healers for their planetary system. This is their service and their gift to all the other Beings. They Joyfully, Peacefully fulfill their Mission.

I am from a remarkable clan of Beings and am Honored to be so. I have been a Healer for eons of time and in different environs. This is who I am.

Suddenly, the CD counts us back to "normal" consciousness—Darn, I'm not ready to come back!

Since I'm expected to join group activities, there was no time to let this all sink in. Later.

* * *

That week at Exploration 27 we also journeyed to the giant crystal at the core of the Earth—yes, that's right. Bob Monroe wrote about going to the center of the Earth in the

1970s. He wrote about a giant crystal there, made from iron. For most of the history of modern science, that idea would have been considered impossible. Geologists thought the Earth's core was made of fiery liquid rock.

Many years ago, I read an article in *The New York Times*, "The Core of the Earth May Be a Gigantic Crystal Made of Iron" by William J. Broad, concerning the understanding that geologists believe the core of the Earth is different from previously thought. (Copyright 1995, *The New York Times*). It would be years before I attended the Monroe Institute, but I had Bob's description of the Earth's core in mind since the scientific understanding of the core was entirely different. I thought, "If Bob Monroe is wrong about what the Earth's core was made of, what else could he have wrong?"

I really wanted to believe all of the incredible things Bob experienced and wrote about in his books were true. But I had doubts about many things, like the Earth's core. Science had been my go-to Belief System—though I didn't want to have Beliefs. I wanted to *Know* information.

As we readied ourselves for the first experience in the second part of Exploration 27, our facilitators told us we would be going to the core of the Earth—to the giant Crystal. By that time, I'd had many dozens of experiences at the Monroe Institute. Much of my doubt about what I might experience there, if it were any different from scientific understanding, was gone with blowouts like "floating out in the Universe."

For years, I thought one way to *Know* something was to experience it. This seemed more solid than believing it or thinking it to be true, based on a given theory. From my point of view, experience trumped Belief or thinking. The scientists had not been to the core. But still—a little Doubt.

However, as I listened to our facilitators guiding us to the Earth's center, I looked around and I was in a huge beautiful crystal. I was in my CHEC isolation unit with my eyes closed, listening to the Hemi-Sync sounds and the voice of one of our facilitators and—I floated in space—inside a clear giant crystal. Stunned, I spent much of that first time in the crystal just experiencing the enormity of it. I don't remember much else, just the wordless encounter with the inside of a massive crystal—a conscious crystal!

We went down to the core of the Earth several times over the next few days. Before one trip, our facilitator suggested that while we were in the Crystal at the core, we might want to check out ley lines around the Earth.

I had heard of ley lines, particularly associated with Chartres Cathedral in France, my "second home." It is believed that ley lines traverse the crust of the Earth and are areas of high energy deemed by indigenous people and many modern individuals to be sacred. Many sacred sites around the globe are thought to be on these high energy lines, including Chartres Cathedral.

Historians say the site the cathedral was built upon is on land of a sacred Druid Healing Site in the middle centuries of the first millennium CE. The Druids were the religious priests of the Celtic people—the earth-based people who inhabited that land before Christianity moved across Europe and usurped the more ancient spiritual practices. In 1979, a well was excavated in the crypt of Chartres Cathedral believed to date back to Druid spiritual and Healing ceremonies. When I visited Chartres, I was fascinated that the well was just such a sacred structure. It was a great idea to check out ley lines to see if one ran under my beloved cathedral. It made sense that the Druids would have a Healing Center on ley lines and that the early Christians of the middle ages would build one of the first Gothic cathedrals on a sacred site.

While I was inside the crystal at the core of the Earth, I sent out the thought that I wanted to see ley lines, in particular, under Chartres.

As I look out from the core crystal, I see the Earth as if I am inside a pure crystalline, transparent globe. I see the "map" of land structures, the oceans, and lakes, all around the Earth. I notice areas where cities are located, as they are more "dense." I see mountain ranges, as they traverse across land and ocean, but, somehow, I see them as if looking up under their bases, into their height and breadth.

Totally engrossed in this view of the Earth, the thought about ley lines and Chartres Cathedral comes back into my awareness. My attention shifts to an area that I know within myself is Chartres. I see two ley lines intersecting under the cathedral and a third one coming up from the core of the Earth, from the crystal I am inside. As I shift my focus around the globe, I see these high-energy lines crisscrossing the Earth. These are more ley lines. I'm not focused on any other particular location on Earth, just taking in the stunning beauty of it all.

The beauty of seeing the Earth in this way was mind-blowing and confirmed the information in books about the existence of sacred, high-energy lines traversing the Earth.

As I continue looking up at the crust of the Earth, I notice other ley lines coming up from the core and connecting along the crust. Then, below me, I notice a ley line that begins at the crystal and, as I follow with my awareness, exits the Earth. It moves out from the crystal as I watch, as if I am observing it grow and expand in the NOW – the line and I are in the Now – not in the past, present or future.

Where is it going? In quick succession—like dominoes falling—it connects with the moon, the sun, all planets, moons and structures of our solar system and on to

– the whole Milky Way Galaxy, connecting every struc-
ture in our galaxy. And then on to every other form in
the Universe – every galaxy, and every structure in the
Universe. What next? I am astounded – as I look at the
whole Universe, Everything in the Universe is connected
to Everything Else by these lines – like an astronomical
giant Web. At each intersection of the Web are sparkling
nodules, extremely bright and beautiful, with each gal-
axy or cluster of galaxies creating a nodule. It is beyond
... description.

As I exist in this Space, in complete awe, there is no
thought, only Awareness; no time, only Now...

I hear the voice on the Hemi-Sync CD, counting us back to normal awareness. *Not* wanting to come back, but back I came. It was very extraordinary and it took me years to integrate it into my understanding of—Life.

I started to understand—Every Structure Is Connected To Everything Else In The Whole Universe. *That* was the answer to the question that popped into my consciousness 25 years earlier. Why were all of these Beings so interested in "front row seats" to witness what was going to happen to the Earth? Earth is *not* just a lowly small planet in a small solar system in one of billions of Galaxies. The Earth, and all of the other structures in the Universe, are connected by energetic lines. And we are connected to the Earth as the source of our physical Life. Therefore, what happens on Earth, or any other heavenly body, happens to everything else in the Universe—and to US.

As I described this to friends, someone said it sounded like the concept of Indra's Jeweled Web. The Web was a metaphor for the existence of the Universe from the Hindu and Buddhist tradition, dating back to the third century CE.

In looking for a description of the Hindu and Chinese Buddhist understanding of Indra's Web, I found a quote from Alan Watts, the well known philosopher who brought Zen Buddhism to the USA:

"Imagine a multidimensional spider web in the early morning, covered with dew drops. And every dewdrop contains the reflection of all of the dewdrops. And in each of the reflected dewdrops, the reflections of all of the other dewdrops in that reflection. And so, ad infinitum. That is the Buddhist concept of the Universe in an image."

During my experience of seeing the cosmic web and its brilliant nodules, it did seem like there were dazzling reflections of each nodule mirrored all of the other nodules—the luminosity of Light.

* * *

Several years later, I saw something that stopped me cold! I was reading an article about the Universe and *there was* a picture just like what I "saw" as the Giant Astronomical Web with the energy lines connected to all of the structures in the Universe. It was a stunning picture of countless purple lines connecting and interconnecting all of the galaxies in a known sector of the Universe. Every galaxy was connected to every other galaxy and where each galaxy or cluster of galaxies was located—a stunning, dazzling Light nodule. Indra's Jeweled Web—each galaxy, a bejeweled treasure.

A little background for context: For most of the 20th Century, astronomers and cosmologists thought they had a pretty good idea how the Universe worked. But, over the last couple of decades, scientists have grappled with a very humbling realization—they know and understand about 5% of what makes up the Universe. Things made of protons, neutrons and electrons, bundled together into atoms. Things that we know of as physical matter.

Something other than physical matter causes galaxies to spin faster than scientists, using their calculations, expected and also keeps the stars in formation within the galaxies. Gravity, as it is understood, is not strong enough to keep stars from being flung out into space, based on the speed with which the galaxies rotate around their centers. No one knows what causes that effect. It is named "Dark Matter"—a placeholder for something yet to be discovered. According to current theories of astronomers and cosmologists, this unknown stuff keeping galaxies together comprises about 27% of the energy of the Universe.

Since the 1920s, we have known that the Universe is expanding in Space in all directions. The question for decades was, would the Universe keep expanding at a constant rate forever, causing a Big Freeze as all galaxies moved farther and farther away from each other? Or would the expansion slow down, stop and the Universe fall in upon itself, causing a Big Crunch.

In the 1990s, two groups of astronomers simultaneously discovered that the Universe was indeed expanding, but faster now than it was some years or centuries or millennia ago. That increase in expansion is continuing to speed up—for forever? Why is that happening? No one knows yet. This effect is named "Dark Energy," as the *cause* yet to be discovered. It makes up 68% of the energy of the known Universe.

So far, Dark Energy and Dark Matter cannot be seen because, it is believed, they do not have protons—light particles. Without protons they do not reflect or refract light. It is unknown what would make these energies visible. So, with all of the great minds in science, physics, astronomy and cosmology, past and present, we, as a species, know only about physical matter—atoms and their smaller constituencies—5% of what comprises the Universe.

The picture I saw that stopped me cold was a computer simulation of what Dark Matter and Dark Energy might look like if we could see it. It is a picture of all of the galaxies within a known sector of Space. In the picture, all were connected by countless cord-like structures with areas of brilliant, glowing light where the galaxies or galaxy clusters existed. It looked *exactly* like a giant web with the galaxies at the intersections of the lines. It was a representation of the connection of *all* the known structures of the Universe—together—just like I witnessed the energetic line exit the Earth and connect to— Everything Else in the Universe.

In Chapter 21 of *Soul Companion*, I describe the astonishing experiences where I saw countless numbers of giant Orbs, each containing a species of Life on Earth. One Orb was my Higher Soul Self. All of those Orbs were connected at a "higher" level and were further connected until there was only ONE. I understood that to be expressing the reality that we, here on Earth, no matter how complex our structure or consciousness, are All One. It is like seeing one Human Being rather than seeing the organ systems that make up the Human, following it down to the individual organs, the cells that make up each organ, the atoms each organelle, the subatomic particles that make up each atom, and so on and on it goes.

The interconnection is not just here on this little planet we call Earth—it is true that the whole Universe, every structure and every Conscious Being on every structure in the Universe is also just One—One Interconnected Being.

Literally—a whole Universe of Dots connected!

Chapter 23
Epilog

After six years of being an Anam Aira, and all I report in *Soul Companion*, I still held two questions. Why did it feel like I was hit with a bolt of lightning when Richard Groves first mentioned the concept of Anam Aira—those special people who escort the dying across the Veil? And, how did I *know* at that moment the work of an Anam Aira was what I needed to do? I wanted those answers!

Toward the end of the sixth year of being both an Anam Cara and Anam Aira, I took a course on Past Life Regression, the practice of working with a hypnotherapist to be verbally guided, called an Induction, into a meditative state to experience other lifetimes—called Past Lives. However, there is no concept of Time from the perspective of the Other Side of the Veil. Therefore, from the "No Time" standpoint, all lives are lived simultaneously—in The Eternal Now. I was intrigued by this notion.

I waited two years to take this course from Rochelle Jaffe, a skilled hypnotherapist in Ashland who directed a well-respected hypnotherapy school for years but was going to retire. This would be her last class.

I thought it might help my clients. I learned from Rochelle how to use hypnosis to help people feel calmer at the end of Life. The Induction I described in Chapter 11 to help Arthur visit the Other Side of the Veil was from her course.

I was excited to learn about helping people connect with their Past Lives. It would enhance my own skills and I would learn from someone I admired.

First, Rochelle regressed some of us. Then we would alternate with a partner so each would take on the role of client, then hypnotherapist. Each time we were in the client role, we had to come up with a personal question.

I knew my first question immediately: *When did the concept of being an Anam Aira get anchored in my Soul?* The question actually surprised me—"anchored in my Soul?" Yes, I had to say, I felt it *was* anchored in my Soul. Nothing had such a profound, sudden and shocking impact on my life as when I heard Richard describe an Anam Aira. From then on, I was driven to do that work, even though it had not really been practiced since medieval times.

Having this weighty question to ask the first time I was induced, I had to calm my excitement at the lunch break. I took a very grounding walk on Rochelle's land above her house in the hills of Ashland. The apprehension left.

Finally, it was my turn. A friend in the regression course led me through the Induction. Initially, I could only sense darkness.

Then, I see light. I open my eyes – not Judy's eyes – the person I am now, in this different Life. I am sitting in a building, a wooden building, a church of sorts. I look down at my lap. I have on a habit – a nun's habit. I am one of perhaps hundreds of nuns. We sit on wooden benches, focused on a teacher – a nun – in front of us. She is teaching us a skill. What skill? I listen. We are learning to meditate—to become very still inside ourselves. It is different than prayer. Focusing internally – not externally, to God. This is very different from what we were used to. Some nuns don't like this way of Being, but we are learning to do Higher work. I will do my very best.

As I focus internally, I am lifted up. I say to myself, "Stay with it – stay with it." I am up and out – out of my body – just like our teacher said would happen. "Stay calm. Calm. Focus."

What do I see? I am in a Heavenly garden – but beyond any beauty I have ever known – the colors are so vivid – trees – plants – flowers I have never seen before. The music – the Heavenly sounds – created by birds, the breeze, the dear animals and who knows what else. The sound comes from every direction. The sounds and sights and sweet smells – the absolute Joy and Love and Peace that is Here. This Place is what our teacher wants us to become familiar with, being Here. We will help people come Here – this most beautiful and sacred Place.

After exploring, our teacher brings us back – back to the church. It is so pale compared to where we just visited. Our teacher says: This is our Mission, our Life Purpose. We help people die peacefully and gently and in a state of Divine Love. If they are scared, we will escort them over to this Divine Place.

Yes, I can do this. It will be my honor for my life.

Our teacher is very Wise, well known in many communities, Loved and Honored. Her name is Bridget. She comes from a neighboring province called Kildare.

I am grateful to be a member of this group. We will be doing this sacred work throughout the land.

My friend inducing me eases me forward in time, in that life-time when I am older.

I walk on a path by myself. I am alone but I am not lonely. I am full of Joy and Peace and Love and oh, the Gratitude that fills my Soul every day. I have a glorious

Mission – to help those afraid of dying – those afraid to let go of this life even as that life is slipping away. I don't know how I became so privileged to be doing this work. Yet, I know I am. I help people know, really know, that we all are Heavenly Souls. We are greater than our bodies – we are Eternal Beings. That is Who we are in our inner most Selves.

I have gone from village to village for many years now, assisting those who need help letting go when their Life is finished. I go over to the Other Side with them when needed. And I live in a state of Ecstasy for a time after coming back from that Other Side. What could be a better life than this? I am truly blessed.

My friend is bringing me back to present – to Now. I am awash with tears of Joy. I now *know* why I focused intensely on the banner of Bridget of Kildare at the front of the conference room during those two years of the apprenticeship, why I felt a deep connection to Bridget when I visited Kildare, Ireland, with Richard a few years after my apprenticeship. I was deeply moved to be walking on the same ground where Bridget was said to have walked. Dear Bridget had been my teacher those many lifetimes ago. She taught me to companion Souls back Home. Just as I do now.

I learned to go to the Special Place that, two millennia later, Bob Monroe would label Focus 27. And now, in the 21st century, I go There to assist others in going Home. And I go There for my own continued growth and great Joy.

I truly know that being a Soul Companion *is* anchored in my Soul—this most precious work—being an Anam Aira. This is my Mission, my Purpose for the rest of this life.

For how many more life times, I don't know. I don't need to know. I trust my Soul's urgings.

The final dots connected.

References

Anam-Aire, Phyllida. *The Celtic Book of Dying*. Rochester VT: Findhorn, 2005.

Broad, William. "The Core of the Earth May Be a Gigantic Crystal Made of Iron." *New York Times*, April 4, 1995.

Buhlman, William. *Adventures Beyond the Body: How to Experience Out-of-Body Travel*. New York: HarperOne, June, 1996.

———. *The Secret of the Soul: Using Out-of-Body Experiences to Understand Our True Nature*. New York: HarperOne, July, 2001.

———. *Adventures in the Afterlife*. New York: HarperOne, June, 2013.

Buhlman, William, and Susan Buhlman. *Beyond the Astral: Metaphysical Short Stories*. Audiobook. Faber, VA: Buhlman, 2019.

Dark matter and dark energy's role in the universe. (2017, January 10). *National Geographic Magazine*.

Greaves, Helen. *Testimony of Light: an Extraordinary Message of Life After Death*. New York: TarcherPerigree, 1969.

Groves, Richard, and Henriette Anne Klauser. *The American Book of Dying: Lessons in Spiritual Pain*. Berkeley, CA: Celestial Arts, 2005.

Howe, Linda. *Healing through the Akashic Record: Using the Power of Your Sacred Wounds to Discover Your Soul's Perfection*. Louisville, CO: Sounds True, 2011.

Kagan, Annie. *The Afterlife of Billy Fingers*. Newburyport, MA: Hampton Roads Publishing, 2013.

Moen, Bruce. *Voyages into the Unknown*. Newburyport, MA: Hampton Roads Publishing, 1997.

Moody, Raymond, MD, with Paul Perry. *Glimpses of Eternity*. Harlan, IA: Guideposts, 2010.

Monroe, Robert. *Journeys Out of the Body*. New York: Anchor Books, 1977.

———. *Far Journeys*. New York: Harmony, 1985.

———. *Ultimate Journey*. New York: Harmony, 1994.

O'Donohue, John. *Anam Cara: A Book of Celtic Wisdom*. New York: Harper Collins, 1998.

Sudman, Natalie. *Application of Impossible Things: A Near Death Experience in Iraq*. Huntsville, AR: Ozark Mountain Publishing, 2016.

About the Author

Judy Hilyard is a retired ICU RN with 47 years experience and two Masters degrees, all sound credentials in Western medicine but not needed for the Afterlife work she is now doing.

At the end of Judy's career, she learned to be an Anam Cara, a soul friend, offering extraordinary counseling to provide a peaceful death for others. During that course, she was shocked into attention when she heard about the ancient practice of being an Anam *Aira*, one who crosses the Veil, not generally practiced today. Judy determined to learn how to cross the Veil between physical life and death to assist souls in their transition.

Soul Companion: A Memoir is the story of what Judy has experienced and learned as she cares for souls on both sides of the Veil. It is joyful work that is healing for all concerned.

And it takes away the fear of dying from those still alive.

Visit Judy Hilyard's website: **www.anamcaracompanion.com**

CPSIA information can be obtained
at www.ICGtesting.com
Printed in the USA
LVHW080319040620
657209LV00001B/151